Shih Tzu

SHIH TZU
AN OWNER'S COMPANION

Wendy M. Brown

The Crowood Press

First published in 1999 by
The Crowood Press Ltd
Ramsbury, Marlborough
Wiltshire SN8 2HR

British Library Cataloguing-in-Publication Data

A catalogue record for this book is available from the British Library.

ISBN 1 86126 194 2

Line-drawings by Annette Findlay

Edited and designed by OutHouse Publishing Service

Printed and bound in Great Britain by Bookcraft (Bath) Ltd.

Contents

Acknowledgements

I am grateful to all those who have helped towards the writing of this book, not least those who have passed on to me over the years the knowledge of the breed which I now seek to share with others. Any virtues which this book may have are largely due to them, the mistakes are my own.

My thanks are due to all those who have so generously provided photographs. Special thanks to Mick Franks, for taking so many photographs exclusively for this book (pages 66, 80, 87, 90, 92, 93, 94, 96, 97, 98, 101, 135, 156, 171, 199 and 208); to Jim Grugan, for permission to use a head study of Ch. Jardhu The Republican for the front cover; and to Animals Unlimited for permission to use a study of Ch. Chelhama De Courcey for the back cover.

My special thanks are also due to the following: to Audrey Dadds, without whose inspiration and encouragement the book would never have been written, and for her advice on the chapter about the history of the Shih Tzu; to Marjorie Divine, for her help with the drawings; to my vet, Robert Mason, B.Vet. Med, MRCVS, for his help with the chapter about ailments and diseases; and to my husband, Alan, for his patience and support during the writing of this book.

1

History of the Breed

The story of the Shih Tzu begins far away in the land of Tibet, a country with a recorded history going back almost 1,500 years. It was in the seventh century that an area of independent tribal rulers was unified into one kingdom, and by the thirteenth century the country was being ruled by a Buddhist religious leader, given the title of Dalai Lama in 1578. This combination of spiritual and political leadership in the form of the Dalai Lama continued until this century: up to the Chinese annexation of Tibet in the 1950s the country was noted for its devotion to Buddhism, with at times nearly a quarter of the inhabitants involved in the various religious orders.

Tibet is a huge plateau, edged by some of the tallest mountains in the world. Its winters are severe, with temperatures down to 14°F (−10°C) in December. There are strong, biting winds and hard frosts, although snowfall is light. In the summer, the daylight temperatures are surprisingly warm for such a high altitude, reaching a maximum of 75°F (24°C), although there is a sharp drop at night during the summer months. During most months there is plenty of sunshine, and the air is dry and pure.

As in so many cultures in our world, the people of this remote and rather mysterious land kept dogs in a domestic environment. There were the large, fierce dogs that were used for guarding, and there were small, shaggy dogs used as companions and as watch-dogs to alert the larger dogs. The small dogs were the ancestors of the Shih Tzu, but it is hard to sort myth from fact in the breed's history. It has been said that the small dogs, 'Lion Dogs', were kept in many of the monasteries throughout the land, and even that they were trained to turn the prayer wheels as part of the daily ritual. I have read of a belief that those monks whose life had been less than exemplary would, in accordance with the Buddhist theory of reincarnation, be reborn as one of the temple dogs. I like to think that the monks, contemplating what might happen to them, would have taken special care of the little Lion Dogs. Sadly, when Audrey Dadds mentioned

7

this tale to a Tibetan monk, he dismissed it as utter nonsense, saying that Shih Tzu were never kept as temple dogs.

Buddhism in Tibet recognized a large number of divine beings, each symbolizing an aspect of life. One of these was the Buddha Manjusri, the God of Learning, who was said to travel with a small Lion Dog that could turn into a full-sized lion and carry him vast distances on his back. Perhaps this is how the small dogs came to be associated with lions, a link that was to continue through their adventurous history. As there were no actual lions in Tibet, the artistic renderings of the animal were often somewhat fantastical. It is hard to be sure whether the Lion Dogs were bred to resemble the drawings and statues of the symbolic lions or if the artists created their 'lions' in the likeness of the little dogs. The snow lion, called the Gang Seng, was considered to be so powerful that he could cause seven dragons to fall out of the sky with one roar. This symbolic lion was believed to have the ability to walk in the clouds, and to speak with the voice of truth and fearlessness.

Despite its inaccessibility, Tibet was not entirely isolated from its neighbours, especially China. From time to time, gifts were sent as tribute to the Chinese emperors, among which were Tibetan Lion Dogs. After a long journey, presumably with the caravans of the traders who travelled over the high mountain passes from one country to the other, the little dogs found themselves in the Chinese imperial palace, in the care of the small army of eunuchs whose job it was to look after the imperial dogs. Here, everything would have been very different, including the climate, for the summers in Peking would have been warm and humid, with a lot of rain, while the winters were very cold indeed, with a minimum temperature as low as 0°F (–18°C) in January. However, the Tibetan Lion Dogs adapted well, as they have done wherever they have gone to live through the centuries.

One imagines that life in the palaces of the Chinese emperors was more than a touch sybaritic. Tibetan Lion Dogs must have been used to a much more Spartan lifestyle, but it is recorded that they settled in and became great favourites of the Manchu emperors. I feel it likely that they were interbred from time to time with the short-faced Chinese breeds – the Chinese Pug or more likely the Pekinese – and that this gave Shih Tzus the characteristics that differentiate them from the Tibetan Lion Dogs that have become today's Lhasa Apsos. (The latter were introduced to Europe via India.) This is purely speculative on my part, and other students of the history of the breed take a different view. In the nineteenth century imperial power in China was held by the

Dowager Empress T'zu Hsi, a formidable lady who was very interested in dogs and who supervised the palace eunuchs in the breeding of the palace dogs, paying particular attention to family lines and colour.

The Lion Dog in Art and Legend

The above account of the history of the Shih Tzu is based on all that I have read on the subject and on my own observation of the various Asiatic breeds. It seems to me the most likely history, and similar versions of the breed's origins have wide acceptance, but there are also other, differing accounts. A definitive history would be very hard to prove, given the mixture of myth and legend that has been handed down to us, although this only adds to the charm of the breed in the eyes of many. For those who are interested, there is plenty more to read about the Lion Dog in Chinese art and culture (*see* Further Reading).

Like many Shih Tzu fanciers in the West, I have been fascinated by the Lion Dog, or Dogs of Fu, models, made in wood, pottery, ivory, jade and a variety of other materials. I count my collection of pottery Lion Dogs as among my most prized possessions, even though they are mostly reproductions rather than originals. They come in pairs, the male with a ball under his paw and the female most typically with her foot planted on a puppy. They are always a talking point with visitors to the house, and over the years people have told me more and more stories concerning them.

'If you ever break one of a pair, you must then smash the other, for if not the surviving dog will grieve and bring bad luck to the home,' said a friend from Sweden. I have also been told that the 'ball' is not a ball at all, but regurgitated food for the puppy. However, since this is regurgitated food from the sacred Lion Dog, it is regarded as containing the secret of eternal life, which is why the male guards it so carefully. One pair of Fu dog models have their skulls covered in tight curls, or so I thought until I was assured that in fact 'the sacred lions sometimes sit quite still for so long when they guard the Buddha at his meditations that snails crawl up and go to sleep all over their heads.' The puppy lies beneath the female's paw, according to one story, in order to suckle milk through the dew-claw: I particularly like that story, because this is the only useful function I have ever heard ascribed to what is otherwise a useless appendage to the Shih Tzu foot.

A New Home in the West

The Shih Tzu is classified as a Chinese breed in Britain because it was originally brought to this country from China. The name 'Shih Tzu', which means something like 'Little Lion' in Mandarin, came from that country with them. Although several dogs were brought to Europe during the pre-war years – to Norway as well as to England– I propose to carry forward my story through the personalities of some remarkable English ladies who had an enormous impact on the breed rights across the world.

Taishan

Lady Brownrigg first obtained a Shih Tzu in 1928, when she accompanied her husband on his posting as Assistant Adjutant and Quartermaster General to the North China command. At this time she must have been about thirty years of age, and was a much-travelled lady as well as being exceedingly fond of birds and animals. When she and her husband returned to England, they brought with them two Shih Tzus, a dog called Hibou and a bitch called Shu-ssa. Both were black and white, and described as small. Shu-ssa was said to have a thick but smooth coat, which stuck out on her head and face so that she looked like a baby owl or alternatively like a chrysanthemum, just as Shih Tzus (especially young puppies) have today. Shu-ssa was mated to Hibou and to a dog called Lung-fu-ssu, which Miss E. M. Hutchins had brought back to Ireland in 1933. It was from the offspring of Hibou, Shu-ssa and Lung-fu-ssu that all the Taishan Shih Tzus were descended, as are so many of our present-day dogs. The weight of these three is known to have been within the range of 12–15lb (5.4–6.8kg), which Lady Brownrigg is said to have considered ideal.

What excitement there must have been at the West of England Ladies' Kennel Society (WELKS) in 1933, when Shu-ssa, Hibou and Lung-fu-ssu were exhibited in a class along with other dogs from Tibet. It was immediately evident that there were great differences between these Tibetan Lion Dogs and those which Colonel and Mrs Bailey had imported from Tibet, which were narrower in the skull and had longer noses. The latter type of dog was eventually to become known and loved as the Lhasa Apso. Other Tibetan dogs, with longer legs, are now known as Tibetan Terriers.

The Shih Tzu (Tibetan Lion Dog) Club was formed and the Brownriggs were instrumental in preparing the first breed standard.

Yangtze of Taishan, sired by Hibou out of Shu-ssa, was one of the first Shih Tzus to be born in England.

By 1934, the breed had been separated from the other small and hairy dogs of oriental origin, and by 1935 the name of the club had changed to the Shih Tzu Club. Shu-Ssa was exhibited at Crufts in 1936, where she took Best of Breed, as did Mai Lin of Taishan in 1937 and Yangtze of Taishan in 1938. The breed went from strength to strength, with over a hundred Shih Tzus registered in 1939; it was granted its own register in 1940, by which time Lady Brownrigg had bred about fourteen litters. But by then World War II had begun, and very few more litters were born during those troubled years. The Taishan Shih Tzus even made their own contribution to the war effort, as the combings from their coats were gathered up and made into knitting wool.

After the war was over, Lady Brownrigg carried on with her work of establishing the Shih Tzu on a sound footing in England, both as Secretary of the Shih Tzu Club and through breeding and exhibiting. The first two Shih Tzus to gain their titles, both owned by Lady Brownrigg, did so in 1949: Ch. Ta Chi of Taishan (by Sui Yan out of Madam Ko of Taishan), bred by Lady Brownrigg, and Ch. Yu Mo Chuang of Boydon (by Yangtse of Taishan out of Hsueh Li Chan of Taishan) bred by Mrs H. Moulton. The other Taishan champions are listed below, with the date when they gained their titles and the name of the breeder or owner if this was not Lady Brownrigg herself:

1950 Ch. Choo Ling (by Sanus Ching-a-Boo out of Sing-Pu) bred by Major-General Telfer-Smollet
1952 Ch. Pa-Ko of Taishan (by Ch. Yu Mo Chuang of Boydon out of Ch. Sing Tsu of Shebo) bred by Mrs S. Bode
1955 Ch. Wang-Poo of Taishan (by Ch. Choo Ling out of Ch. Pa-Ko of Taishan)

Lady Brownrigg was not always in agreement with developments within the breed, such as the decision to introduce Pekinese blood and the attempt to start a new club for the miniature Shih Tzu, and where she opposed she did so forcefully. Even when she was no longer so active in the breed, she was still concerned for the welfare of the Shih Tzu, and she would go to the championship shows to talk to the exhibitors, not hesitating to give a frank opinion on the merits or otherwise of their dogs.

I cannot help wondering what would have happened if General Sir Douglas Brownrigg had not been posted to China early in his career.

Lady Brownrigg, her cook Mrs Doig, and some of the Taishan dogs. In the foreground is Ch. Yu Mo Chuang of Boydon.

12

Ch. Wang Poo of Taishan, descended from the Queen Mother's Choo-Choo, was himself much used at stud.

Would fate have thrown Lady Brownrigg into the path of the Shih Tzu in some other way? Fate certainly seems to have played a part when a lady called Gay Garforth-Bles, later Gay Widdrington, saw eight Shih Tzus being exercised in Thurloe Square in London. This was in 1939, when the Brownriggs were living there, and the dogs were being exercised by Mrs Doig, their cook.

Lady Brownrigg's last litter of puppies.

13

Lhakang

Gay Widdrington bought her first Shih Tzu from Lady Brownrigg shortly after that sighting in Thurloe Square. This was a black and white puppy bitch called Mee-Na of Taishan, and although she was originally purchased with the idea that Gay would like a little dog as a companion, Mee-Na set her owner off on a course that would lead her to become one of the best-known figures in the breed, so that today, wherever in the world people gather to talk 'Shih Tzus', you may be sure that they will be familiar with the name 'Lhakang'.

By her own admission, Gay was somewhat casual in her approach to dog owning in the early days, with the result that Mee-Na's first

Gay Widdrington's Mee-Na of Taishan, aged twelve, with three of her grandchildren.

Mee-Na of Taishan, Gay Widdrington's first Shih Tzu, was very fond of rock climbing!

Gay Widdrington with a group of Shih Tzus in 1960, including (top left) Ch. Maya Wong of Lhakang and (top right) Ch. Mao Mao of Lhakang.

litter was the outcome of a liaison with a Dachshund, not something that Gay confessed to Lady Brownrigg until much later. Modern breeders may be a little shocked to learn that Mee-Na's first Shih Tzu husband was her own father, Yangtze of Taishan, but it must be remembered that the choice of available sires was extremely limited in those early days. It was Gay's awareness of this that led her to import a dog from Norway in 1947, Pjokken av Dux; unfortunately this dog died in quarantine, but Mee-Na did subsequently have a litter sired by Lady Brownrigg's Ch. Choo-Ling, a great-grandson of the Shih Tzu which the Duchess of York had received as a gift from Norway in 1933. The Duchess (later the Queen Mother) called her Shih Tzu Choo-Choo, and he was bred out of two of the original imports to Norway from China. It is said that King George VI thought him well named as 'Choo-Choo' because he made noises just like a train. Choo-Choo was said to be rather too long in the nose and to have an overshot jaw, but he was used at stud none the less.

Those first Lhakang litters were the forerunners of many more. Indeed, Gay Widdrington has bred more than a hundred litters in all, over a period of nearly fifty years. The list of Lhakang champions overleaf shows how this kennel has competed at the highest level in the breed over a thirty-year period, a remarkable achievement. The name of the owner or breeder is shown where this was not Gay herself, and each name is preceded by the year in which the title of champion was gained.

1951   Ch. Mao Mao of Lhakang (by Lyemun of Taishan out of Mee-Na of Taishan)

1951   Ch. Shebo Tsemo of Lhakang (by Pu of Oulton out of Lindi Lu of Lhakang) owned by Mrs S. Bode

1953   Ch. Tensing of Lhakang (by Ch. Yu Mo Chuang of Boydon out of Ch. Mao Mao of Lhakang) owned by Mr and Mrs K. B. Rawlings

1955   Ch. Maya Wong of Lhakang (by Ch. Yu Mo Chuang of Boydon out of Ch. Mao Mao of Lhakang)

1956   Ch. Lily-Wu of Lhakang (by Ch. Yu Mo Chuang of Boydon out of Ch. Mao Mao of Lhakang) owned by Mr and Mrs K. B. Rawlings

1958   Ch. Elfann Ta-To of Lhakang (by Yenmo of Lhakang out of Chen Mo of Lhakang) bred by Mrs Widdrington together with her mother, Mrs L. Mather, and owned at the time of gaining her title by Mrs Murray Kerr

1958   Ch. Shu She Yu of Lhakang (by Ch. Yu Mo Chuang of Boydon out of Ch. Mao Mao of Lhakang) owned by Mrs A. E. Haycock

1960   Ch. Tien Memshib (by Bimbo out of Mu Ho) bred by Mrs T. Morgan

1960   Ch. Tzu Ann of Lhakang (by Jo Jo of Lhakang out of Mei-Hua of Lhakang) owned by Mrs A. O. Grindey

1961   Ch. Jou-Li of Lhakang (by Bimbo out of Ch. Maya Wong of Lhakang) owned by Mr P. Beeley

1964   Ch. Soong of Lhakang (by Chuangste of Lhakang out of Ching Yo of Elfann)

1970   Ch. Jen Kai Ko of Lhakang (by Sing Hi of Lhakang out of Jessame of Lhakang) owned by Mrs E. Fox

1984   Ch. & Finnish Ch. Lhakang Cassius (by Tor Ra Lon out of Cherubim of Lhakang) owned by Mrs Y. Brooker

Ch. Shebo Tsemo of Lhakang, owned by Gay Widdrington.

A Lhakang family group in 1950. Left to right, Ch. Mao Mao of Lhakang, two of Mao Mao's daughters and Mee-Na of Taishan.

Gay's outstanding contribution to the establishment of the breed has been through her breeding programme. She has always been an innovative breeder, never fearing to introduce new bloodlines to widen the gene pool but always cleverly breeding back into her own line thereafter, thus preserving the best from the very earliest strains that came to England. Her appreciation of the value of fresh bloodlines has continued since those early days when it was so essential to establish the breed. In 1989 she bred a litter using frozen semen imported from Norway, choosing to do this specifically in order to counteract what she regarded as a potential danger from an hereditary problem in the breed, namely the increasing incidence of umbilical hernias. Sadly, the Kennel Club did not agree to register this litter, so it has not

Ch. Soong of Lhakang.

A group of exhibitors at the 1957 Scottish Kennel Club Show in Edinburgh. Left to right, Mrs Murray-Kerr with Ch. Elfann Ta-To of Lhakang, Mrs Widdrington with Lhakang Mimosa of Northallerton, Mrs Sommerfield, Mrs Arnott and Miss and Mrs Ross.

served the purpose that Gay had in mind, but this is a good example of the efforts this dedicated lady has always been willing to make for the advancement of the Shih Tzu.

During the post-war years, Gay Widdrington joined with Lady Brownrigg in developing the Shih Tzu Club as a strong influence in the breed. Later, in the 1950s, she was involved in the formation of a second club, the Manchu Shih Tzu Society, with the aim of promoting the smaller type of Shih Tzu (for which Gay had a particular appreciation). The Kennel Club did not agree to the division of the breed into two sizes, and so the Manchu was given official status only on condition that it promoted the welfare of all sizes of Shih Tzu – as it does to the present day.

As I write, Lhakang remains the longest-established kennel of Shih Tzus, with an influence stretching right round the world. It has particular impact in Scandinavia, where Lhakang breeding lies behind literally scores of champions.

Elfann

Freda Evans, a breeder of Pekinese and to a lesser extent Griffons, acquired two Shih Tzus in May 1952, purchasing them from Mrs

Int. Nord. Ch. Lhakang Celandine, bred by Gay Widdrington, owned by Major Borre Hasle in Norway, where she was Shih Tzu of the Year in 1986 and 1987 and produced 11 champion children.

Widdrington's mother, Mrs L. Mather. Gay Widdrington has told me that these two grew too big and strong for Freda's taste, and they were therefore passed on to new homes. Freda then acquired two more Shih Tzus, the bitch Elfann Fenling of Yram and her liver-coloured daughter, Channe Tu of Elfann. She had decided that what the breed needed was the introduction of Pekinese blood, and so it was that she carried out the famous (or infamous) Peke cross in October 1952. The fact that the cross had been carried out by a newcomer to the breed and without consultation with the breed club seems to have caused a great deal of bad feeling, especially as it was not generally agreed that the faults Miss Evans was seeking to correct were particularly prevalent in the breed as it then stood. These faults included being too large and leggy, and having too much length in the nose and bad pigment.

Freda chose a black and white Pekingese male, one with rather straight legs, to mate to her small Shih Tzu bitch, Elfann Fenling of Yram (sired by Ch. Shebo Tsemo of Lhakang out of Chin Ling of Hunjao). The best bitch in the litter resulting from this match was mated to a pure-bred Shih Tzu, in fact one of Lady Brownrigg's males, Ch. Choo Ling. The late Thelma Morgan, who took a bitch

19

Shih Tipsee of Elfann, born 1954 (by Fu Chan of Elfann out of Elfann Fenling of Yram).

called Mu-Ho from the third cross, described her as 'more Shih Tzu than she was Peke, yet I felt there was a still a lot of work to do to before one could say that all the points that went to make the Shih Tzu Standard were not only visible but were there in depth'.

Mu-Ho's progeny, four generations down the line, were accepted by the Kennel Club as pure-bred Shih Tzus, although it is interesting to note that in America Shih Tzus were not accepted as such until seven generations after the initial cross. Today, the vast majority of British Shih Tzus carry the Peke cross far back in their pedigrees, and so the debate about the wisdom of what occurred is largely academic. The gene pool is much larger now, so there should be no reason for anyone to attempt such a course again.

Undeterred by the furore she had raised, Freda Evans went on to become a very successful breeder of Shih Tzus, although she exhibited only one to its title in England herself, as the list opposite shows:

A group of typical 'Elfanns' in 1962. Left to right, Li-Shan, Ching-Yo, Ying-Mei and Min Yuenne.

Freda Evans with Ch. Shiraz of Ellingham at the Leicester Show in 1964.

1964   Ch. Shiraz of Ellingham (by Tackla Sahib of Lhakang out of Michelcombe Crystal of Clystvale) bred by Lady Haggerston
1968   Ch. Golden Peregrine of Elfann (Sing Hi of Lhakang out of Golden Bobbin of Elfann) owned by Mr and Mrs A. Leadbitter
1970   Ch. Greenmoss Golden Sunbeam of Elfann (Int. Ch. Greenmoss Golden Peregrine of Elfann out of Elfann Sunshine of Greenmoss) owned by Mr and Mrs A. Leadbitter
1974   Ch. Golden Summertime of Elfann (Ch. Greenmoss Chin Ki of Meo out of Golden Bobbin of Elfann) owned by Mr T. Hoyle
1975   Ch. Elfann Golden Posy of Lansu (Ch. Zeus of Bridgend out of Chin-Eelee of Elfann) owned by Mr T. Hoyle
1975   Ch. Golden Heidi of Elfann (Int. Ch. Golden Peregrine of Elfann out of Elfann Sunshine of Greenmoss) owned by Mr T. Hoyle

Miss Evans was approved as a championship show judge and served as a committee member of the Manchu Shih Tzu Society. She exported puppies to both America and Canada, where they enjoyed great success in the show ring. For a few years in the 1960s she went to live with the Widdringtons in Northumberland, and Gay Widdrington has expressed her admiration for Freda's expertise

21

Golden Bobbin of Elfann, at six months (by Tregye Peng Yu out of Shantung of Witches Knowe).

with the dogs. At the age of eighty-three, never having previously left England and never having flown, she set off for America to judge at the Shih Tzu Fanciers of Greater Miami First Specialty Show. This was in 1975, and was made possible by the kindness of the late Tom Hoyle and his wife Sylvia, who accompanied Freda and who organized everything for the journey. After her death, the Kennel Club permitted Freda's adopted daughter Jenny Taylor, together with Sylvia Hoyle (now Rawlings) of the Lansu affix, to continue to use the Elfann name.

Today, nearly forty years after the event, it is hard to estimate exactly how things might have been had the Peke cross not taken place. Even though I was at school when Miss Evans decided to cross the Peke with the Shih Tzu, I still heard strong feelings aired on the subject when I came to be involved with the breed myself. Looking back on it now, I think that what caused most controversy was the way in which it was carried out, considering that (so far as I know) nobody had considered the option in the years before Miss Evans involved herself in the breed. Above all, I wonder why she did not consult with the breed club and the experts therein, and carry out the cross-breeding with official club approval. Was this because she knew that such approval would not be forthcoming? Audrey Dadds, a much respected breeder who knew Lady Brownrigg well, and indeed who took in the latter's remaining two Shih Tzus after her death, says that we cannot be certain whether Lady Brownrigg allowed her own dog to be mated to the first-generation Peke cross bitch because she accepted the wisdom of the decision or simply because she wanted to make the best of a situation That she could neither approve nor change.

Some of the very faults which Freda Evans cited as the reason for her decision continue to occur to this very day: we still find puppies that are leggy, oversized or too long in the nose cropping up. We also see a bowed 'Chippendale' front occurring from time to time, and this is sometimes referred to as a 'Peke' front to this very day. We seek to eliminate these faults nowadays by selection, making sure that only sound and typical animals are used to produce the next generation.

I have concentrated on the story of these three formidable ladies because of their great influence on the breed. There were, of course, many other devotees of the Shih Tzu to whom we owe our gratitude for their efforts in securing the future of these little dogs; their work has been particularly important as it can be assumed that the breed has died out in China since the Communist government banned keeping dogs as pets. In 1980, hearing that Sir Peter Allen had visited Tibet, I wrote to ask him if he had seen any Shih Tzus or Lhasa Apso type dogs whilst there. He replied that they had seen none such in Lhasa.

Many of those who brought home these little dogs served abroad with the armed forces or with the diplomatic service. Among the best known were Henrik Kauffmann and his wife, who took three Shih Tzus to Norway in 1932. Others came to England after the war with Major-General Telfer-Smollet in 1948 and Mr and Mrs Morris a year later. These and other pioneers of the breed, Miss Hutchins in Ireland, Mrs Bode and Mrs Fowler in England, must be paid the tribute that is due, for it was they who gave us the breed to cherish. A story could be told about each of them.

The Golden Age

The 1950s and 1960s were something of a Golden Age for the Shih Tzu in Britain. Although Lady Brownrigg was no longer so active in the breed, both Gay Widdrington and Freda Evans continued to make their presence felt, and judged the breed regularly, so there was continuity from the early days. Among the English kennels that entered the breed during the period, three in particular have been important, not only because of the quality of the dogs they bred and owned but also because of the influence of their stock overseas, and their dedication to the breed right up to the present day. For those new to the phraseology of the dog world, I should explain that 'kennels' refers to breeders rather than the commercial establishments that make a living from selling and boarding dogs – in fact, all three of the kennels discussed below keep their dogs in a domestic situation. They are the Antarctica kennel of Ken and Betty Rawlings, Arnold and Jeanne Leadbitter's Greenmoss, and Audrey Dadds' Snaefell. All of these breeders have earned their place in the history of the breed both by the length of time over which they have played a part, and by their significant contribution to the welfare of the Shih Tzu through their support for the breed clubs.

Antarctica

The Antarctica kennel of Ken and Betty Rawlings has been the most successful in the history of the breed in Britain, exhibiting winning dogs for over thirty years and showing skill in choosing puppies from the litters of other breeders as well as breeding their own winners. Two notable successes among many were that of winning Best in Show at the WELKS Championship Show in 1960 with Ch. Pan Wao Chen of Antarctica, and that of campaigning Ch. Kuire Hermes of Antarctica to the position of breed record holder, a record he continued to hold until 1988. Ken Rawlings served for more than forty years as Chairman of the Shih Tzu Club, a record not only for Shih Tzus but also perhaps for any club in any breed. Betty was also unstinting in giving her time and experience to the clubs, and during the years when she and I served together as committee members of the Manchu Shih Tzu Society, I remember her advice to the club as being invaluable. After Betty's death, Ken became less active in the show ring, but he continues to take an active interest in the affairs of the breed to this day, being Patron of the Shih Tzu Club of Wales and the South West. British champions bred or owned at Antarctica include the following:

1953   Ch. Ling-Fu of Shuanghsi (Lyemun of Taishan out of Wu-Ling of Shuanghsi) bred by Mrs J. Hopkinson
1953   Ch. Tensing of Lhakang (Ch. Yu Mo Chuang of Boydon out of Ch. Mao-Mao of Lhakang) bred by Mrs G. Widdrington

1956 Ch. Lily-Wu of Lhakang (Ch. Yu Mo Chuang of Boydon out of Ch. Mao-Mao of Lhakang) bred by Mrs G. Widdrington

1956 Ch. Yi Ting Mo of Antarctica (Ch. Shebo Tsemo of Lhakang out of Tang of Oulton)

1957 Ch. Yano Okima of Antarctica (Perky Ching of the Mynd out of Ch. Sing Tzu of Shebo)

1958 Ch. Sindi-Lu of Antarctica (Ch. Yi Ting Mo of Antarctica out of Chao Meng-Fu of Antarctica) bred by Mrs A. L. Dadds

1960 Ch. Suki of Maesvyn (Ch. Yi Ting Mo of Antarctica out of Yet Ming of Maesvyn) bred by Mrs M. Cope

1961 Ch. Kuan Ti of Antarctica (Ch. Yi Ting Mo of Antarctica out of Ch. Ling-fu of Shuanghsi)

1962 Ch. Pan Wao Chen of Antarctica (Ch. Yi Ting Ho of Antarctica out of Dan Gau of Shanghoo) bred by Mrs St John Gore

1964 Ch. Shang Wu of Antarctica (Ch. Pan Wao Chen of Antarctica out of Chia of Antarctica) owned by Mr J. Moody

1964 Ch. Susie Wong of Antarctica (Shebo Wen Yin of Lhakang out of Ch. Suki of Maesvyn)

1965 Ch. Chi-Ma-Che of Antarctica (Jungfaltets Jung Ming out of Elfann Tara of Clystvale) bred by Mrs M. Longden

1966 Ch. Kuang Kuang of Antarctica (Ch. Chi-Ma-Che of Antarctica out of Sing-Tzu of Antarctica)

1966 Ch. Ling Fu of Antarctica (Longlane Telstar out of Domus Yanda) bred by Miss E. L. Bennett

1967 Ch. Antarctica Chan Shih of Darite (Ch. Chi-Ma-Che of Antarctica out of Fu Chi of Darite) bred by Mrs Copplestone

1968 Ch. Fleeting Yu Sing of Antarctica (Ch. Pan Wao Chen of Antarctica out of Fleeting Banwee Ming) bred by Mrs M. Garrish

1970 Ch. Cha-Saki of Antarctica (Ch. Antarctica Chan Shih of Darite out of Gina of Antarctica)

1970 Ch. Che Ko of Antarctica (Ch. Antarctica Chan Shih of Darite out of Ch. Shang Wu of Antarctica)

1970 Ch. Ya Tung of Antarctica (Ch. Fleeting Yu Sing of Antarctica out of Susanah of Antarctica)

1971 Ch. Antarctica Don Juan of Telota (Ch. Fleeting Yu Sing of Antarctica out of Ch. Domese of Telota) bred by Mrs O. Newson

1972 Ch. Kuire Hermes of Antarctica (Ch. Ya Tung of Antarctica out of Duchess of Telota) bred by Mrs J. Johnson

1972 Ch. Mu T'ang of Antarctica (Choo Yau Fong of Antarctica out of Antarctica Chan Sophie of Akaben)

1973 Ch. Antarctica Ta T'ung Fu (Ch. Ya Tung of Antarctica out of Chih Shih of Antarctica) bred by Miss K. Willeby

1974 Ch. Su Tung Po of Antarctica (Ch. Ya Tung of Antarctica out of Lu Che of Gorseycop) bred by Miss K. Willeby

1976 Ch. Sandi Quai Lu of Antarctica (Ch. Kuire Hermes of Antarctica out of Yar-Min T'sing) bred by Mrs J. Broadbent

1978 Ch. Shou Shang of Antarctica (Ch. Kuire Hermes of Antarctica out of Ch. Antarctica Ta T'ung Fu)

1979 Ch. Philwen Mi Boi of Antarctica (Ch. Sandi Quai Lu of Antarctica out of Si-tsung of Antarctica) bred by Mr and Mrs Behan

1986 Ch. Harropine Charka Khan at Antarctica (Sistasu Silver Bullet out of Harropine Odyssey) bred by Mrs D. and Mr M. Harper

Greenmoss

Jeanne and Arnold Leadbitter have not only had great success in the show ring themselves, but have also contributed to the success of kennels in other countries where the Greenmoss Shih Tzus have been imported. A few examples of Greenmoss champions overseas will serve to demonstrate this. In Australia there was Austral. Ch. Saffron of Greenmoss who, mated to Austral. Ch. Chin Wang of Greenmoss, produced three Australian Champions in her first litter. In America, Mr and Mrs Wing of Florida owned Am. Ch. Greenmoss Gilligan; in Canada there was Can. Ch. Greenmoss Golden Frolic of Elfann, while Ch. Greenmoss Soket Tumi and Ch. Greenmoss Saki's Legacy gained their titles in South America. Success for the Greenmoss dogs in Europe has included Int. Ch. Greenmoss Tit Fer Tat (owned by A. Berggren) and Int. Ch. Greenmoss Promise To Bee (owned by B. Sabel), both in Sweden, and Int. Ch. Greenmoss Song of Bee owned by Danielle Ulrich in France.

If I had to single out one of the many famous Greenmoss dogs, it would be Ch. Greenmoss Chinki of Meo, not only for his success in the show ring but also for his prowess as a sire since he was the father of a dozen or so champions. In 1980 he received the Award of Merit from the American Shih Tzu Club, an award given to any Shih Tzu that has sired six or more American champions.

Both Jeanne and Arnold have given much of their time to the breed clubs over the years, Arnold having served as Chairman of the Manchu Shih Tzu Society and Jeanne holding the same post for the Northern Counties Shih Tzu Club.

Greenmoss British champions include the following:

1964 Ch. Mei Saki of Greenmoss (Greenmoss Yu Li Ching of Wyndtoi out of Sasha Ming of Wyndtoi) bred by Mrs E. Roberts

1966 Ch. Greenmoss Chin Ki of Meo (Choo T'sun of Telota out of Elfann Maya Wen of Ricksoo) bred by Mrs V. Reynolds

1966 Ch. Katrina of Greenmoss (Ch. Greenmoss Chin Ki of Meo out of Mei Lu Lu of Wyndtoi)

1968 Ch. Golden Peregrine of Elfann (Sing Hi of Lhakang out of Golden Bobbin of Elfann) bred by Miss E. M. Evans

1970 Ch. Greenmoss Golden Sunbeam of Elfann (Int. Ch. Greenmoss Golden Peregrine of Elfann out of Elfann Sunshine of Greenmoss) bred by Miss E. M. Evans

1971 Ch. Chin Ling of Greenmoss (Ch. Greenmoss Chin Ki of Meo out of Hsiang Chieh of Liddesdale) bred by Mrs J. Mangles

1971 Ch. Fei Ying of Greenmoss (Int. Ch. Golden Peregrine of Elfann out of Brownhills Yu Honey)

1971 Ch. Ko Ko Saki of Greenmoss (Ch. Jen Kai Ko of Lhakang out of Ch. Mei Saki of Greenmoss)

1973 Ch. Greenmoss Soket Tumi (Ch. Greenmoss Chin Ki of Meo out of Ch. Greenmoss Golden Sunbeam of Elfann)

1973 Ch. Wysarge Chin Ki Tuo of Greenmoss (Ch. Greenmoss Chin Ki of Meo out of Franwil Kiki Dee) owned by Mrs E. M. Johnson

1974 Ch. Greenmoss Glory Bee (Int. Ch. Greenmoss Golden Gaylord of Elfann out of Greenmoss Chantilly Lace)

1976 Ch. Greenmoss Chinki's Fling (Ch. Greenmoss Chin Ki of Meo out of Ch. Ko Ko Saki of Greenmoss)

1979 Ch. Greenmoss Bee in a Bonnet (Ch. Greenmoss Glory Bee out of Wysarge Jade Lotus Bud)

1980 Ch. Greenmoss Bees Knees (Ch. Greenmoss Glory Bee out of Wysarge Jade Lotus Bud)

1983 Ch. Greenmoss Surely Bee (Ch. Greenmoss Glory Bee out of Wysarge Jade Lotus Bud)

1984 Ch. Greenmoss Yu Tu (Greenmoss Knee Breeches out of Ch. Greenmoss Bee in a Bonnet)

1992 Ch. Greenmoss Praise Bee (Ch. Camllien Touch of Class out of Greenmoss Daisy Tuo)

Snaefell

The name of Audrey Dadds is known to Shih Tzu fanciers across the world, not only for the quality of her dogs, which have been successful in Europe and as far afield as Australia and South Africa, but also

*One of Audrey Dadds'
Snaefell puppies in the 1960s,
showing the type and
classical markings for which
she looks in a puppy at eight
weeks. (Photo: L. Young.)*

for her prolific writing on the breed. She has always been willing to give her time and advice to help the new owner, and still is today. Among the best known of the Snaefell dogs was Ch. Newroots Nanki Poo of Snaefell, one of the champion sons of the Leadbitters' Ch. Chin Ki and himself the sire of a champion line. Audrey has had an exceptionally long association with the Shih Tzu Club, of which she is now President. Snaefell British champions include:

1963 Ch. Li Ching Ku of Snaefell (Yibbin of Antarctica out of Missee Lee of Snaefell)
1963 Ch. Su Si of Snaefell (Tzu-Hang of Snaefell out of Chung of Snaefell)
1972 Ch. Newroots Nankipoo of Snaefell (Ch. Greenmoss Chin Ki of Meo out of Ho Yan of Newroots)
1980 Ch. Buttons of Snaefell (Ch. Zeus of Bridgend out of Snaefell Flame) bred by Mrs I. May
1983 Ch. Snaefell Charm (Ch. Buttons of Snaefell out of Newroots Pitti Sing of Snaefell)

*Audrey Dadds, with Ch. Newroots Nankipoo of Snaefell, winning
Best of Group at Southampton in 1994. The judge was Bill Siggers.
(Photo: L. Young.)*

1983 Ch. Snaefell Imperial Imp (Ch. Newroots Nankipoo of Snaefell
out of Snaefell Queen of the Snow)
1984 Ch. Snaefell Katrina of Janmayen (Ch. Newroots Nankipoo of
Snaefell out of Ch. Snaefell Charm) owned by Mesdames Pickburn
and Duke
1991 Ch. Snaefells Limited Edition (Am. Ch. Din Ho Rupert T. Bear
out of Snaefell Irma La Douce)
1992 Ch. Snaefell Imperial Rose of Janmayen (Keltina Fan Kang of
Snaefell out of Ch. Snaefell Imperial Imp) owned by Mesdames
Pickburn and Duke

Together with Taishan, Lhakang and Elfann, the kennel names of
Antarctica, Greenmoss and Snaefell will be found behind many of the
Shih Tzus across the world today. Anyone who searches through
the names at the back of his dog's pedigree will be very likely to find
one or more of these.

Snaefell Oswald, owned and bred by Audrey Dadds. Born in 1993, he is a great-grandson of Ch. Newroots Nankipoo of Snaefell, with the American lines of Am. Ch. Din Ho Rupert T. Bear on the maternal side.

Popularity

From about 1970 onwards, the most potent influence on the Shih Tzu was no longer that of any individual breeder but the effect of the growing popularity of the breed itself. It was increasingly favoured as a pet dog as it became more available, and at the same time it was gaining more and more acceptability as a show dog in England and continental Europe, and also in America where the breed had finally been registered as separate from the Lhasa Apso in 1969. While breed registrations with the Kennel Club during the 1950s had averaged just 81, in the 1960s the average rose to 480 and in the 1970s to 1,460, with a peak in 1979 of more than 2,000. The names of many of the kennels that rose to fame in those years will be referred to in later chapters.

Popularity has a danger for any breed in that it attracts mass producers or 'puppy farmers', and this breed has been no exception. This causes particular distress to the true devotee of the Shih Tzu because of the breed's character and temperament, both of which make it particularly unsuited to kennel life or to an existence as a breeding machine, deprived of human companionship. One sad outcome of the population explosion was the need to set up a means of caring for dogs which no longer had homes for one reason or another, and this has led to an organized structure of 'rescue' groups up and down Britain today. Exemplary work is done by these groups in re-homing Shih Tzus where possible, but it is regrettable that it should be necessary in the first place. Those of us who can remember when it was rather difficult to obtain a Shih Tzu cannot help wishing it was not quite so easy nowadays.

The increase in numbers and popularity has also led to more and more breed clubs being formed to promote the well-being of the Shih Tzu. In addition to the two national clubs, the Shih Tzu Club and the Manchu Shih Tzu Society, mainland Britain now has regional clubs for Wales and the South West, for the Northern Counties and for Scotland. The Irish Republic has its own club, and there is also the Ulster Club in Northern Ireland. There are Shih Tzu clubs throughout Europe, including the Internationaler Shih Tzu Club, based in Germany, and the Swedish Shih Tzu Club. The American Shih Tzu Club was not established until the mid-1960s, although the breed had been recognized in Canada as early as 1935. The last few years have seen a number of imports from both these countries to the UK, the impact of which on the British Shih Tzu has yet to become fully apparent.

In the show ring, the increased popularity of the breed has led to much stiffer competition and has attracted skilled exhibitors from other breeds, who have brought new standards of presentation with them. It is probably in the area of coat preparation and care that the greatest changes have taken place over the last twenty years. Modern Shih Tzus are indeed glamorous creatures in the ring, especially in America, although European exhibitors are catching up in this respect. As I observe from the ringside today, they just do not appear to be the same breed as the shaggy, rather unruly little show dogs that so captivated me when I returned from living abroad in the 1960s. Happily, however, they remain possessed of exactly the same lively temperament and eccentric character as before, even though they are so well groomed and schooled for their public appearances.

31

2

The Breed Standards

An official Breed Standard is published for each breed that is recognized by the kennel club of a country. This is a word picture of the ideal dog of that breed, and provides the blueprint for breeders to use when producing the next generation, as well as for judges at dog shows to use as the standard against which the dogs exhibited are to be measured. Sometimes, as for example when watching Crufts on television, people are unable to understand how a judge can seem to be comparing an Irish Wolfhound with, for example, a tiny Chihuahua, but of course this is not what is really happening at all. What the judge actually does is to compare each of those dogs with his mental picture of the ideal for its breed, in order to put first that dog which is nearest to his imagined picture of perfection. All Breed Standards deal with the parts of the dog point by point, but a dog is a good specimen only when all these parts are balanced one with another. Most dogs are like the curate's egg, 'excellent in parts', but it is only when the whole animal is harmoniously balanced that you start to see something really special.

The Shih Tzu Standard given opposite is the latest version to be approved by the Kennel Club, as revised in 1986; before that there were three versions, the longest standing and most influential of these being in force from 1958 to 1986. This previous version of the Breed Standard is shown in full at Appendix I and is valuable study material for the serious student of the Shih Tzu. All the breed clubs then in existence were involved in the consultation process preceding the revision that took place in 1986, and after each committee had come to an agreement over the details, Mr Rawlings of the Antarctica Shih Tzus hosted a conference at which representatives of each club came together to co-ordinate a unified approach. This stands out in my mind as one of the times when all concerned really co-operated and supported one another, in contrast to other occasions when the mood in the breed has been rather more divisive and sectional. It was an important moment in the history of the breed in Great Britain.

UK Breed Standard

(Reproduced by kind permission of the Kennel Club.)

General Appearance

Sturdy, abundantly coated dog with distinctly arrogant carriage and chrysanthemum-like face.

Characteristics

Intelligent, active and alert.

Temperament

Friendly and independent.

Head and Skull

Head broad and round, wide between eyes. Shock-headed with hair falling well over the eyes. Good beard and whiskers; the hair growing upward on the nose, giving a distinctly chrysanthemum-like effect. Muzzle of ample width, square and short but not wrinkled; flat and hairy. Nose black but dark liver in liver or liver-marked dogs, and about 1in (2.5cm) from tip to definite stop. Nose level or slightly tip-tilted. Top of nose leather should be on a line with or slightly below lower eye rim. Wide-open nostrils. Down-pointed nose highly undesirable, as are pinched nostrils. Pigmentation on muzzle as unbroken as possible.

Eyes

Large, dark, round, placed well apart but not prominent. Warm expression. In liver or liver-marked dogs, lighter eye colour is permissible. No white of eye showing.

Ears

Large, with long leathers, and carried drooping. Set slightly below the crown of the skull; so heavily coated that they appear to blend into the hair of the neck.

Mouth

Wide, slightly undershot or level. Lips level.

Neck

Well-proportioned, nicely arched. Sufficient length to carry head proudly.

Forequarters

Shoulders well laid back. Legs short and muscular with ample bone; as straight as possible, consistent with broad chest being well let down.

Body

Longer between withers and root of tail than height of withers; well-coupled and sturdy; chest broad and deep, with shoulders firm and back level.

Hindquarters

Legs short and muscular with ample bone. Straight when viewed from the rear. Thighs well-rounded and muscular. Legs looking massive on account of wealth of hair.

Feet

Rounded, firm and well-padded, appearing big on account of wealth of hair.

Tail

Heavily plumed, carried gaily well over back. Set on high. Height approximately level with that of skull to give a balanced outline.

Gait/Movement

Arrogant, smooth-flowing, front legs reaching well forward; strong rear action and showing full pad.

Coat

Long, dense, not curly, with good undercoat. Slight wave permitted. Strongly recommended that hair on head is tied up.

Colour

All colours permissible; white blaze on forehead and white tip to tail highly desirable in parti-colours.

Weight and Size

10–18lb (4.5–8.1kg). Ideal weight 10–16lb (4.5–7.3kg). Height at withers no more than 10½in (26.7cm). Type and breed characteristics of the utmost importance and on no account to be sacrificed to size alone.

Faults

Any departure from the foregoing points should be considered a fault, and the seriousness with which the fault should be regarded should be in exact proportion to its degree.

Note: Male animals should have two apparently normal testicles fully descended into the scrotum.

American Breed Standard

(Reproduced by kind permission of the American Kennel Club.)

General Appearance

The Shih Tzu is a sturdy, lively, alert Toy dog with long flowing double coat. Befitting his noble Chinese ancestry as a highly valued, prized companion and palace pet, the Shih Tzu is proud of bearing and has a distinctly arrogant carriage with head well up and tail curved over the back. Although there has always been a considerable size variation, the Shih Tzu must be compact, solid, carrying good weight and substance. Even though a Toy dog, the Shih Tzu must be subject to the same requirements of soundness and structure prescribed for all breeds, and any deviation from the ideal described in the Standard should be penalized to the extent of the deviation. Structural faults common to all breeds are as undesirable in the Shih Tzu as in any other breed, regardless of whether or not such faults are specifically mentioned in the Standard.

Size, Proportion, Substance

Size Ideally, height at withers is 9 to 10 inches, but not less than 8 inches nor more than 11 inches. Ideally, weight of mature dogs is 9 to 16 pounds. **Proportion** Length between withers and root of tail is slightly longer than height at withers. The Shih Tzu must never be so high stationed as to appear leggy, nor so low stationed as to appear dumpy or squatty. **Substance** Regardless of size, the Shih Tzu is always compact, solid, and carries good weight and substance.

Head

Head Round, broad, wide between eyes, its size in balance with the overall size of the dog, being neither too large nor too small. *Fault:* Narrow head, close-set eyes. **Expression** Warm, sweet, wide-eyed, friendly and trusting. An overall well-balanced and pleasant expression supersedes the importance of individual parts. Care should be taken to look and examine well beyond the hair to determine if what is seen is the actual head and expression rather than an image created by grooming technique. **Eyes** Large, round, not prominent, placed well apart, looking straight ahead. Very dark. Lighter on liver-pigmented dogs and blue-pigmented dogs. *Fault:* Small, close-set or light eyes. **Ears** Large, set slightly below crown of skull; heavily coated. **Skull** Domed. **Stop** There is a definite stop. **Muzzle** Square, short, unwrinkled, with good cushioning, set no lower than bottom eye rim; never downturned. Ideally, no longer than 1 inch from tip of nose to stop, although length may vary slightly in relation to overall size of dog. Front of muzzle should be flat; lower lip and chin not protruding and definitely never receding. *Fault:* Snipiness, lack of definite stop. **Nose** Nostrils are broad, wide and open. **Pigmentation** Nose, lips, eye rims are black on all colors, except liver on liver-pigmented dogs. *Fault:* Pink on nose, lips or eye rims. **Bite** Undershot. Jaw is broad and wide. A missing tooth or slightly misaligned teeth should not be too severely penalized. Teeth and tongue should not show when the mouth is closed. *Fault:* Overshot bite.

Neck, Topline, Body

Of utmost importance is an overall well-balanced dog with no exaggerated features. **Neck** Well set on, flowing smoothly into shoulders; of sufficient length to permit natural high head carriage and in balance with height and length of dog. **Topline** Level. **Body** Short-coupled and sturdy with no waist or tuck-up. The Shih Tzu is slightly longer than tall. *Fault:* Legginess. **Chest** Broad and deep with good spring of rib; however, not barrelchested. Depth of ribcage should extend to just below elbow. Distance from elbow to withers is a little greater than from elbow to ground. **Croup** Flat. **Tail** Set on high, heavily plumed, carried in curve well over back. *Fault:* Too loose, too tight, too flat or too low set a tail is undesirable and should be penalized to extent of deviation.

Forequarters

Shoulders Well-angulated, well laid-back, fitting smoothly into body. **Legs** Straight, well-boned, muscular, set well apart and under chest, with elbows set close to body. **Pasterns** Strong, perpendicular. **Dewclaws** May be removed. **Feet** Firm, well-padded, point straight ahead.

Hindquarters

Angulation of hindquarters should be in balance with forequarters. **Legs** Well-boned, muscular, and straight when viewed from rear, with well-bent stifles, not close set but in line with forequarters. **Hocks** Well let-down, perpendicular. *Fault:* Hyperextension of hocks. **Dewclaws** May be removed. **Feet** Firm, well-padded, point straight ahead.

Coat

Luxurious, double-coated, dense, long and flowing. Slight wave permissible. Hair on top of head is tied up. *Fault:* Sparse coat, single coat, curly coat. **Trimming** Feet, bottom of coat and anus may be done for neatness and to facilitate movement. *Fault:* Excessive trimming.

Color and Markings

All are permissible and to be considered equally.

Gait

The Shih Tzu moves straight and must be shown at its own natural speed, neither raced nor strung up, to evaluate its smooth, effortless movement with good front reach and equally strong rear drive, level topline, naturally high head carriage, and tail carried in gentle curve over the back.

Temperament

As the sole purpose of the Shih Tzu is that of a companion and house pet, it is essential that its temperament be outgoing, happy, affectionate, friendly and trusting towards all.

Interpretation and Comparison

General Appearance

I like the American Standard here because it is more explicit than the British. Read together, they give a good impression of this arrogant little dog as he is seen in the show ring. The coat flows as the dog moves; and if the action underneath is correct and sound, the strength and weight of the dog should give a strong, driving action. A Shih Tzu on the go has been described as a 'ship in full sail', a description which compares the billowing of the topknot and tail plumes to the sails on a ship; but it is a ship surging forward rather than merely floating, and most certainly not wallowing.

Head

The head is of great importance in this breed. No matter how well constructed or how soundly he moves, a dog that is lacking in type as far as the head and expression are concerned cannot be considered an excellent specimen of the breed. For there to be width between the forward-facing eyes, it is necessary for the head to be broad. This, together with the required roundness of the skull, gives a larger head than that of the Lhasa Apso, although the size is very much a matter of proportion and should be considered in relation to the overall size of the dog. The muzzle, which is the foreface (the part in front of the eyes), should be of ample width, square and short but not wrinkled,

| Pekingese | Shih Tzu | Lhasa Apso |

Although the breeds may at first glance seem to be similar, the differences, especially in the heads, are quite distinctive.

in great contrast to that of the Pekingese. A pointed (snipy) muzzle gives the dog a weak expression, and if the muzzle lacks width there is less likely to be room for the teeth to be set correctly.

The length of the nose is described as about 1in (2.5cm) from stop to tip, allowing for a tiny bit more on a large dog and a fraction less on a small one. The nose placement is very important and can make a huge difference to the head of a Shih Tzu: when you look at the head straight on, the tip of the nose should be on a level with the bottom of the eye, not lower than this. If the nose falls away towards its tip this

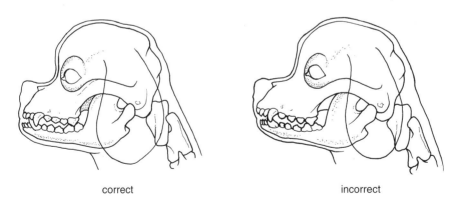

correct   incorrect

When the head is correctly shaped the nose is short and slightly tilted upwards at the tip, whereas the long nose and flatter skull gives a non-typical expression.

is a serious fault, giving an untypical expression and probably leading to a shallow stop. The stop (the indentation between the eyes where the nasal bone and the skull meet) must be 'definite' but not excessively deep.

The colour of the nose and lips must be unbroken, as must that of the eye rims, since flesh marks in this area can spoil the look of the dog, and it should be black, except on liver-coloured dogs when it may be liver. I am often asked what exactly 'liver-coloured' is: it is a colour defined by the Kennel Club as 'deep brown, chocolate'. In Britain, Shih Tzus with this colouring have always been less popular, and indeed are not often seen in the show ring.

Eyes

When the Standard asks for large eyes, this does not mean the larger the better as they must be balanced in proportion to the width of the skull. Certainly, a small eye will mar the expression. It should be noted that the eyes should not be prominent: this means that they should not bulge, as such an eye would be ugly as well as prone to injury. The phrase 'No white of eye showing' did not appear in the earlier versions of the Standard, indicating that this had previously been less of a problem but by 1986 it had come to be regarded as something that needed watching. I remember that one of the bitches I owned at that time, who usually had lovely full dark eyes, had a tendency to flare them when she was alarmed; when this happened her expression was quite changed, and her whole face became dominated by these huge 'pop-eyes', each surrounded by white like a poached egg.

Something which is difficult to describe is the 'warm expression' in the eye, but anyone who becomes familiar with the breed should need no elaboration on this point: it is very much a feature of the Shih Tzu that he will look up at you with just that characteristic soft-eyed gaze which this phrase attempts to capture. Some people have described it as a 'melting gaze', and have said that this is truly a dog with his soul in his eyes.

Mouth

The British Standard is not informative about dentition. The normal complement of teeth in the canine species is forty-two, consisting of incisors, canines, premolars and molars. In the UK, most attention is paid to the twelve incisors (six in the upper jaw and six in the lower), these being the teeth at the front between the sharp canines at the corners. Judges and breeders in continental Europe pay a lot of attention to the back teeth as well.

The jaw must be wide in order to accommodate the incisors in a straight line, or else these teeth will either be jumbled together (as if God threw them in from a distance, as one of the old breeders once said to me) or curving outwards in a spoon shape – both of these are faults, as is a mouth with one or more incisors missing. Some of the most successful Shih Tzus in the British show ring have had less than six incisors in the lower jaw, indeed quite a few champions have had only four. These champions have been exhibits that have excelled in almost every other point, to the extent that judges have been willing to forgive the fault of incomplete dentition, or else they have gained their titles at a time when the standard of competition was not at its highest.

The incisors must either meet edge to edge, or be slightly undershot, with the teeth in the lower jaw projecting just a little beyond the line of those in the upper. Both of these arrangements mean that the incisors cannot be used as effectively as they are in the more conventional canine scissor bite. Twenty-five years ago, it was not unusual to see a Shih Tzu with an extremely undershot jaw, sometimes by as much as half an inch, and this was accepted then so long as the teeth did not show when the mouth was closed. The condition

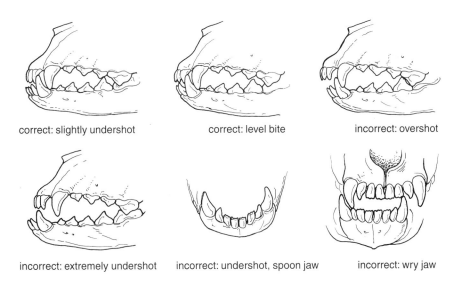

correct: slightly undershot   correct: level bite   incorrect: overshot

incorrect: extremely undershot   incorrect: undershot, spoon jaw   incorrect: wry jaw

Jaw formation in the Shih Tzu.

41

when the top front teeth overlap those in the lower jaw is called 'overshot' and is a serious fault, as is a wry mouth where the upper jaw is misaligned with the lower.

Neck

Both American and British Standards emphasize that the length of the neck must be just enough to contribute to the overall balance of the dog and enable the head to be carried proudly. This clearly indicates that those who consider it a case of 'the longer the better' are quite mistaken.

Forequarters

It is here that we see one of the points of greatest divergence between the Standards, for in America the legs are described as straight whereas in the UK they are required to be as straight as possible, 'consistent with broad chest being well let down'. When the British Standard was revised in 1986, none of the breed clubs was happy to accept the suggested wording of 'legs straight'. Many felt that to require the legs to be absolutely straight might result in a narrow, terrier-type front, hence the resulting phrase, which is something of a compromise. The presence of a broad, deep chest is likely to result in a slight curve to the foreleg, but this must not be so pronounced that the whole front is bowed and the feet either turned in towards each other or alternatively turned out. A bowed front with turned-out feet is commonly known as a 'Queen Anne' front, and is a particular cause of incorrect front movement and rolling in front. The description of the

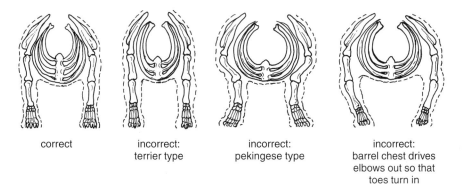

| correct | incorrect: terrier type | incorrect: pekingese type | incorrect: barrel chest drives elbows out so that toes turn in |

Forequarter functions.

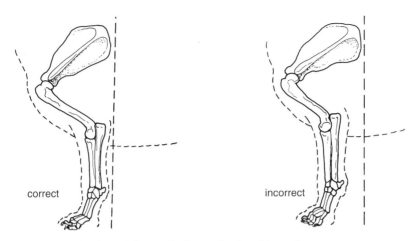

A correct shoulder blade angle brings the foot under the withers. An incorrect length to the upper arm brings the foot too far forward, even if the shoulder blade is at the correct angle.

front legs as straight was in the Standard drawn up in 1948, but was later taken out because, Audrey Dadds tells us, 'it was realized that the legs were not straight when compared with those, for example, of a terrier'.

This almost straight leg is described as short (it must be short since the height at the withers must not exceed 10½in or 26.7cm) and muscular with ample bone. Insufficient substance, especially as far as bone is concerned, continues in my opinion to be a problem with the breed. Ample bone is always something I look for when judging, remembering the dictum I was taught in my early days in the breed, namely that a Shih Tzu should always be heavier than he looks. Much of this weight will come from the bone; it does not mean that one is looking for a fat dog.

The shoulder is well laid back. This layback – the angle at which the scapula or shoulder blade slopes back from the vertical when viewed from the side – will affect not only the Shih Tzu's appearance but his movement. An upright shoulder will give the dog a stuffy appearance, even if he does have the correct length of neck, and it will also inhibit the forward swing of the front leg. Usually this leads to the dog compensating in his rear action, with the result that he 'toddles' with a shortened stride. To balance the layback of the shoulder blade, the humerus, or upper arm, must be of sufficient length to bring the elbow back into position under the withers: an upper arm that is too short will once again lead to a stilted movement, although thisfault is not always apparent to the eye because of the wealth of coat.

Body

The body is longer between the withers (the highest point of the body, immediately behind the neck) and the root of the tail than it is high at the withers – that is, it is rectangular, not cobby or short in the back. As to how much longer than high the back must be, the answer is, as with most things, a question of balance. The longer-legged dog will have a proportionately longer back, the low-to-ground specimen less. The breadth and depth of chest has already been mentioned in connection with the front assembly, and this must be accompanied by a sturdy and well-coupled body, which is to say that the ribs go well back along the body so that there is not too long a loin between them and the hindquarters. A long loin can be a cause of weakness and may lead to back problems for the dog, especially in later life. The

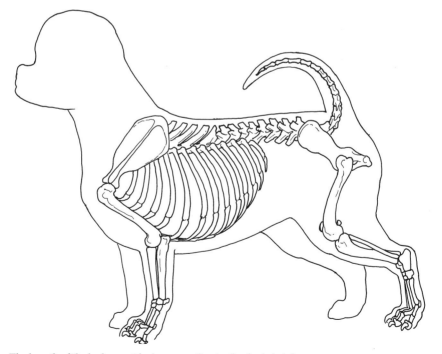

The length of the body must be in proportion to the dog's height.

Shih Tzu does not have a waist, as I have already stressed, nor should he be tucked up underneath. The topline must be level when the dog is on the move as well as when he stands.

Hindquarters

Above all there must be a length of leg and a degree of angulation that match those of the forequarters; otherwise the topline will either rise or fall from the withers to the root of the tail, and movement will also be faulty, something I shall come to later. The American Standard stresses the importance of well-bent stifles, and I suspect that those who drew up the British version did not see stifles as much of a problem. Perhaps the incidence of cow-hocks or bowed rear legs has been greater in the breed, and so emphasis was laid on the fact that the rear legs must look straight when viewed from the rear.

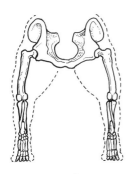
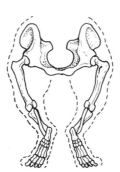
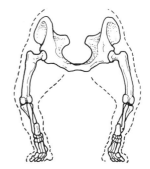

correct   incorrect: cow hocked   incorrect: too bowed and wide

Hindquarter formations.

Tail

Both the placement of the tail on the body and the carriage of the tail are very important to the overall appearance of a Shih Tzu. Tails that are set on too low are unlikely to be carried correctly up over the back in the desired loose curve, and so will not be level with the skull as would be desired. The carriage, even with a correctly set tail, can vary enormously, from quite flat on the back, through the 'teapot handle' curve to the wildly flagging style in which the appendage never touches the back at all except where it is fastened on. The tail is one of

45

| correct tail, set on high and carried in a 'teapot handle' shape. Only the coat falls to the side | incorrect tail, with root of tail set on too low – tail cannot be carried up and over the back as required by the Standard. | incorrect tail, lying flat on the back – gives an unbalanced effect |

Tail carriage.

a dog's means of communication, so tail carriage can vary with mood. A dog that is frightened may drop his tail, while a wary or defensive dog may tighten his tail down onto his back a little. Sometimes it is only when the weight of the fully adult coat furnishing arrives that a high tail settles into position, and equally that same weight of coat can flatten a tail that had seemed well carried when it was less heavily furnished.

Gait/Movement

Many of the features of the Shih Tzu in action have already been mentioned with regard to the other points of the dog. I have referred to the problem of stilted movement both when it is caused by faults in shoulder placement and when it is a result of lack of balance between front and rear quarters. When the dog is striding out, well co-ordinated and balanced, he will show his pads behind as he goes away from you. From the side you will see that the topline remains level and is not bobbing up and down. I wish we had in the British Standard what is written in the American, namely that the Shih Tzu should neither be raced nor strung up in the show ring, for both habits can give such a wrong impression of the dog. Racing means moving the dog along so fast that the hind legs converge and create the impression that the dog is moving close behind. As for stringing up, which is to say holding the lead very tightly with no slack at all, the arrogance of this breed on the move comes from its head carriage, and a dog on such a tight lead cannot show himself to advantage.

Coat and Colour

The texture of a Shih Tzu coat is not described in the Standard, which may be just as well since texture can vary a lot from dog to dog. It has been likened to the texture of human hair, but that doesn't help a lot as humans also have a huge variety of hair types. In the 1948 Standard there was an interesting phrase, since gone, which stated 'looks harsher than it feels to the touch'. Although the long and dense coat must not be curly, a slight wave is permitted, and is more often found in the stronger type of coat than the soft. This is a breed with a double coat, although the soft undercoat is concealed by the flowing long hairs of the top-coat. No one who has to groom a Shih Tzu regularly will be unaware of the undercoat, especially if it is very woolly and inclined to mat up.

All colours are allowed with this breed. Indeed, it would be a great shame if we were ever to lose the great variety that we presently have: there are parti-colours, gold and white, black and white, brindle and white and so on; as well as the solid-coloured coats, which may or may not have a black mask. There is no special virtue given to one colour rather than another, but almost everyone I know has their own favourite. The Standard does not mention mis-marking, and so this cannot be considered a fault, but it has to be said that a Shih Tzu can look rather odd with uneven markings on his head, for instance with one side of the moustaches white and the other coloured, or with the hair on the ears of different colours. I do not remember one so marked ever doing exceptionally well in the show ring.

Weight and Size

In America the height from the ground is more specifically defined than in the UK, and the lower weight limit is set at 1lb (450g) less, with the upper weight limit being 2lb (900g) lower. This seems to me entirely consistent with the fact that the breed is classified as a Toy in one country but most emphatically not in the other. The British Standard adds to the defined limits of 10–18lb (4.5–8.1kg) that the ideal is 10–16lb (4.5–7.3kg). With such a wide range of weights permitted, there can be no excuse, as the Standard goes on to say, for sacrificing type and breed characteristics to size alone.

A dog touching the upper weight limit permitted will, at 18lb (8.1kg), be very nearly twice the weight of one that weighs just 10lb (4,5kg), yet both are correct. Many breeders, including me, feel that for a bitch to weigh in at the top of the range is less acceptable than for a dog, and vice versa at the bottom of the weight scale. But we have to remember that the Standard does not make a distinction between the sexes in this way. Shih Tzus are not weighed in the show ring as, for example, some Dachshunds are, and so it is up to the judges to make an informed guess based on experience. I do recall one English judge, years ago, who used to lift each dog down from the table in what seemed to be a helpful and gentlemanly gesture to the exhibitors. In fact, he was doing it to check the weight of each dog, being very concerned at the time that the dogs were getting too large. You will note that I say 'too large' rather than 'too heavy', because this judge's fear was that the dogs were large without substance, that they lacked the necessary bone and were not therefore as heavy as they looked.

The Whole Dog

Ask any judge or breeder to write notes about the Breed Standard and each will probably lay a slightly different emphasis on the points therein. The fact that individual interpretations of a Standard differ is the main reason why there is so much variation in the judging of any breed, so that a dog can win one day and yet go down the line a week later. None the less, when an exceptional dog enters the ring he will be put up (awarded first place) by the majority of judges under whom he is exhibited in any one year.

Although I began this chapter by calling the Breed Standard a blueprint, we can see that this is not in fact such a good description. The Shih Tzu was not bred to resemble the Standard, for originally the Standard was written down to describe the salient points of what was then considered to be the best sort of Shih Tzu. Over the years the breed has changed, and so has the Standard. This process will probably continue in the years ahead, although perhaps the wider use of video cameras, together with the ease with which modern fanciers are able to travel the world, may tend to keep type more fixed.

The danger with considering the Breed Standard section by section lies in losing sight of the important fact that the dog as a whole must have an overall balance. A Shih Tzu might have excellent points when considered feature by feature and yet look quite wrong, simply because he lacks the all-important virtue of balance. In assessing the merits of dogs, we must never lose sight of the fact that the whole may be greater than the sum of the constituent parts.

3

Choosing a Shih Tzu

Before you set off to acquire your first Shih Tzu, or indeed any other type of dog, you need to ask yourself a couple of questions. The first is whether you are able to make the necessary financial commitment, remembering that the purchase price of a puppy is the very least of this. There will be the cost of food, routine injections, bedding and coat care products, all of them necessary throughout the dog's lifespan, which you can reasonably hope to be from twelve to fifteen years. Even if you are lucky enough to obtain an extremely fit animal, he is likely to need veterinary attention from time to time, especially in old age. One thing I can guarantee after all my years of dog ownership is that vets' bills keep going up and up, year on year.

The second question is whether you can make the required commitment of time. Your dog will need regular walking, grooming, bathing and, especially if he is the only one in the household, play and companionship. Remember that the dog is a pack animal, so it is not really fair to force him to spend his time in solitude. If everyone in the family is out at work all day, it is going to be extremely difficult to house-train a puppy and to teach him what is and what is not acceptable behaviour. Where there are very young children, they should never be left with a dog unsupervised.

Why a Shih Tzu?

The Shih Tzu has become one of the most popular breeds of dog, both in Europe and America, with registrations of the breed at the Kennel Club reaching 4,000 and more in the 1990s. This is hardly surprising when you consider his appearance and character. Perhaps you were first attracted by the sight of this arrogant and confident little dog, striding along with his tail held high as if he owned the street. And of course the expression of a Shih Tzu is quite beautiful, with his bright, shining eyes sparkling at you above a black tilted nose, framed with those flowing moustaches and surmounted by the waving hair of the topknot. One look at that whiskery little face, and I confess I was lost to this breed.

Certainly this is a lovely breed to live with, and the personality of the Shih Tzu never ceases to fascinate. One minute he is playing the fool, the next gazing at you like a solemn oriental potentate, then leaping onto your lap for a cuddle or a snooze, and then off to look for mischief again. The doorbell rings, and you have a fierce little Lion Dog, ready to defend you with his life. Start to prepare some food, and watch his antics as he tries to wheedle a titbit from you – they are usually successful. Even housework is a game to the Shih Tzu, who joins in whether you wish it or not. Watching a group of Shih Tzus at play is often much more entertaining than anything on television. They are robust and energetic for their size, and certainly not a toy-like dog, even though they are classified with the Toy breeds in some countries, including America.

The Shih Tzu lives to a good age for a dog, averaging about twelve years or so, with some living much longer: I have heard of them reaching the grand old age of seventeen or eighteen. It is also a healthy breed overall, plagued with very few hereditary conditions that might cause concern. True to the description in the Breed Standard, Shihs Tzu tend to remain active and alert well into old age, and while young they enjoy lots of activity and exercise. For the latter they like nothing better than a good walk, and where there are two or more they will also exercise themselves by playing and running together so long as there is space in the garden for them to do so. Generally speaking, Shih Tzus get on well together, but there are occasions when they can quarrel, often through jealousy over food or a toy. They are very intelligent and benefit from having a variety of

Shih Tzus have been clowns from the very beginning. Miss Hutchins, who lived in Ireland in the 1930s, sent Lady Brownrigg this snapshot of her dogs.

Yu La of Lyre is described by her owner, Francis Hickey, as showing all the Shih Tzu traits of playfulness, wilfulness, stubborness and naughtiness, whilst also having a very placid temperament in the show ring.

Ch. Khumar China Silk of Darralls with an Afghan friend. (Photo: J. S. Gurney.)

51

toys to play with; if they do not they can become bored, and a bored Shih Tzu will soon find some mischief to get up to.

One of the possible disadvantages of Shih Tzus is that they are not generally very obedient and rarely if ever slavishly so. If you call a Shih Tzu to come to you, he is quite likely to pretend to be momentarily deaf, or (as one of mine always does) to give you the 'in a minute' glare and just carry on with whatever he thinks is more important at the time. For this reason it is important to have a garden that is quite escape-proof, and also to be very sure of your dog before you let him off the lead away from home. Some Shih Tzus have proved the exception to this rule, but I have not owned one. As a good example of this lack of biddability, I had one especially naughty puppy who thought by the time he was six months old that his name was 'NO!' – with the result that sometimes, when I was admonishing another of the dogs, he would appear at my side with furiously wagging tail and a 'did you call?' expression on his face. I attribute his naughtiness to more than just usual puppy disobedience, since he has a dominant nature and grew up to become the leader of the pack, even usurping his bossy father to achieve this position. Despite this, Ricky is today a lovable and loving Shih Tzu. Now a veteran, he maintains his

Darralls China Snapdragon, owned and bred by Dorothy Gurney.
A coat of good texture is relatively easy to keep in order. (Photo:
J. S. Gurney)

top-dog status whilst still being perfectly willing to be used as a toy by the latest puppy arrival in the household. Of course, to this day he occasionally suffers from the aforementioned selective deafness.

My description of the Shih Tzu as a breed inclined to be stubborn is based on my personal experience. In fairness I should add that not everyone who owns a Shih Tzu would agree with me. Indeed, in America some Shih Tzus have won the title of Companion Dog Excellent (CDX), which just goes to show what can be done. To win CDX, the dog must have reached a high level of achievement in the American Kennel Club Obedience Trials.

Another potential disadvantage of owning a Shih Tzu is the coat, which can be a problem. The long hair can be trimmed, or even cut right off, and this happens quite often, but I do not see the point of buying a breed that is noted for the beauty of its coat and then to get rid of its crowning glory. You should at least be prepared to try to keep your dog's coat in good condition and free from tangles, and if you succeed you will be amply rewarded by the admiration a long flowing coat will attract. So long as the coat is of a good texture, like that of human hair and neither too woolly nor silky, it should not really be too arduous to keep it in good order.

Choosing a Puppy as a Pet

When you visit a litter of puppies with a view to purchase, you should always be able to see them with their mother. The dam cannot be expected to be in perfect and full coat, but you may be able to see if the hair is of good texture: should the coat of the dam be woolly, for example, it is possible that the puppies will have inherited that coat and consequently be very difficult to keep free of mats. More importantly, try to assess the dam's temperament, bearing in mind that she may be a little on edge when in the presence of strangers who are taking such an interest in her babies.

A healthy puppy should be bright-eyed and bushy tailed, almost literally. The skin and coat should be clean, and neither the nose nor the eyes should be runny. Watch out for the problem of pinched nostrils which, if severe, can cause a puppy to snuffle almost constantly. Beware of buying a puppy from a litter that is being kept in dirty conditions, as the latter suggests bad husbandry. Although you could always agree to buy such a puppy subject to a veterinary check, I doubt this would really be advisable: by the time you have taken him home and been told by your own vet that he really is a poorly little thing, you will probably feel so sorry for him that you keep him anyway.

Puppies must be eight to twelve weeks of age, at the very least, before they are ready to leave the breeder. At this age, their personalities will have begun to develop, and it is possible to see which puppy in a litter is more outgoing and which less confident, although if there is one very dominant puppy the others will become much more extrovert once they are removed from their bossy sibling. As far as Shih Tzus are concerned it is a fallacy that the bitch is more affectionate and biddable than the male, and the sex of a puppy is no indication of his character. Some people will have a strong opinion about what colour they are looking for in their dog, but I would recommend paying more attention to health and temperament. A breeder should know the puppies really well by the time you go to make your choice, and some breeders will make a real effort to match the puppy with the new owner, so listen to their advice. Ask the breeder if any of the puppies have hernias (*see* Chapter 11) and, if there is one, enquire whether it is serious enough to require surgery later on.

As can be seen from the Breed Standard, the Shih Tzu comes in a wide range of weights, so that the largest specimen can be almost twice the weight of the smallest. Depending on your lifestyle, you may prefer to seek out a puppy that is going to tend to the top or the bottom of the weight scale, in which case it is important to explain this to the breeder.

Be prepared to be questioned quite intensely by the person who is selling you your puppy. Caring breeders will always want to ensure that their litters end up in absolutely the right homes, and if some of the questions seem to verge on the impertinent, please remember that it is right and proper that the interests of the puppy should be put ahead of your feelings. If you go to see a litter of puppies before they reach the age at which they can leave home, you may wish to reserve one of them, in which case it is customary to offer a deposit towards the cost of the puppy.

You will be given a pedigree with your puppy, showing his family tree for four or five generations, and the official Kennel Club registration papers either at the time of purchase, or later in the post if the breeder has not got them through when you call to collect your puppy. When breeders sell a Shih Tzu puppy to a pet home, they will often choose to endorse the registration so that the puppy may not be shown or bred from; the reasons for this will be explained to the purchaser. A diet sheet is also provided, and this should be followed carefully for the first week or so to avoid the tummy upsets that so often follow a sudden change in diet.

Choosing a Puppy for Show

When you are selecting a puppy for show, all of the foregoing advice still applies, but you will have much more homework to do. This involves reading the Breed Standard, together with books about the breed, and then going to several shows, preferably championship or club shows because there will be many more Shih Tzus to see at such events. When watching Shih Tzus at shows, do not concentrate on the winners, which you will discover vary from show to show according to the judge, but sit quietly at the ringside and mark in the catalogue those dogs that truly appeal to you. Then, back home, study the catalogues to see if a pattern is emerging. Are you tending to prefer the stock from one particular breeder, or that which is sired by a certain stud dog? If so, approach the breeder, or the owner of the stud dog, and talk to them about your needs. If you approach them at a show, make sure it is at a convenient time and especially not just at the moment they are going into the ring.

Details of the shows and breeders in your area can be obtained from any of the breed clubs, although it may be necessary to travel further afield to find the puppy of your dreams. If you find that you have been drawn to one coat colour more than another, the club secretaries will also know which breeders specialize in the colour you prefer.

It can be very difficult to choose one Shih Tzu puppy from a litter! Three enchanting Jardhu puppies at the age of six weeks.

Sooner or later, you may be invited to view litters of puppies. The problem here is that an eight- or nine-week-old puppy looks very different from those seen at shows, since a puppy must be at least six months old in order to attend a show. The advice of an experienced breeder can be invaluable, as it is based on knowledge of the bloodlines and of how puppies from previous litters have developed. Take any claims of guaranteed show quality with a large pinch of salt: these are nonsense, for many of the show points (for example dentition) are not measurable at an early age. You would need a crystal ball to be quite sure how any puppy is going to turn out. The most any honest breeder is likely to claim for a puppy at about ten weeks of age is that he is 'promising', so long as nothing goes wrong – which, of course, it can and sometimes does. The name of the game at this stage is to try to pick a puppy that does not have any major faults, as it is certainly no good hoping things will improve – they rarely do. This is where all that study of the breed at shows, and of the Breed Standard at home, should come in useful, since many of the show points can be assessed simply by watching the puppies carefully.

The head is of great importance in this breed. Look for width in a puppy's skull, with wide-spaced dark eyes and a well-placed nose. There should also be height to the skull, so look for a puppy with a good round, domed head. No white of eye should show when the puppy is looking straight at you; in some lines this is known to fill in later, but if there is a marked 'poached egg' effect (with white of eye showing all around the pupil) I would be a bit sceptical of any claims that this will completely disappear as the puppy grows. The nose should be well pigmented, and there should be no noticeable flesh-marked areas on the muzzle or eye rims. Look for a short nose, level with the bottom of the eyes and maybe tilted at the tip, but certainly not sloping down away from the skull. The jaw should also be wide, and upper and lower jaw should meet either on the level or with the lower jaw very slightly undershot. The degree by which the lower jaw is undershot is likely to increase as the puppy grows. Unfortunately, the conformation of the first set of teeth – which can be seen at this age – is not an indication of how the second set will be (*see* Teething, Chapter 10). The fault most commonly found is that of missing incisors: there should be six incisors in each jaw.

As you look at a young puppy in outline, you will see the balance between height on the leg and length of back. Sometimes a puppy that is quite low to the ground may come up on the leg as he ages, although one that is leggy will almost certainly always be so.

Snaefell Loatse of Chaomin, showing a balanced outline at eight weeks of age.

Similarly, a short-backed youngster may lengthen with maturity, whereas one which is too long in the back will remain so. The tailset can be assessed at an early age, but not necessarily the carriage of the tail, because when they are teething many puppies carry their tails in quite untypical ways for a week or two.

Looking down from above, a Shih Tzu should be broad and look sturdy all the way back to the tail, not waisted behind the ribs like a Pekinese. Avoid picking a puppy that is too narrow all through, because unless he develops the required breadth he will always look too long in the back, even if he isn't. Check for hernias (*see* Chapter 11), as the presence of these can affect the puppy's suitability for show or for breeding.

Movement is difficult to assess in a baby puppy, although it is possible to detect faults such as a bowed front (not to be confused with one that is just a bit slack) or an upright shoulder. Watch out for a straight stifle, which is unlikely to improve very much.

The coat develops at a different rate in different lines, but generally look for dense and strong growth. Although the Breed Standard does not specify mis-marking as a fault, this can cause the dog's expression to appear wrong if, for example, the whiskers are white on one side of the nose and coloured on the other. Uneven markings could be a disadvantage in the show ring if they are so placed that they could distract the eye of the judge.

When all this has been taken into account, many experienced breeders will say that there is something about one puppy that will make him the 'pick of the litter'. Call it charisma, 'attitude', or what you will, there is something just that bit extra that will draw the eye to one dog rather than another, and this applies at any age. Lucky is

Dorothy Gurney imported Gemihs Yump To The Moon With Darralls (bred by Gunmarie Swedenhall) after seeing him as a puppy in Sweden. (Photo: Gunmarie Swedenhall.)

Spike, a puppy from the first litter to be sired by Gemihs Yump To The Moon With Darralls. (Photo: Yvonne Hyde.)

the exhibitor who finds a good Shih Tzu with this extra something about it: with care and hard work, he or she is surely onto a winner!

When choosing 'pick of litter', whether it be from your own home-bred puppies or from someone else's, it is worth bearing in mind just one thing. The hard truth is that the second- or third-best puppy from a really top-quality litter can be a considerably better show prospect than the best puppy from a less distinguished bunch of pups. This is sometimes hard to face up to when it is your own little litter that is being assessed, but to accept that your own much loved and patiently reared babies are not really out of the top drawer as far as show points are concerned is a big step on the way to improving your stock in the future.

Choosing a puppy is a big decision, since you are going to take this bundle of charm into your home and live with it for a decade or more, but when you are selecting a puppy specifically with the intention of showing then the decision becomes even more crucial. Don't be in too much of a rush to buy the first puppy you are offered. If you have any doubts, go away and think about it, or make arrangements to see another litter and compare them in your mind. But please do not go from breeder to breeder on the same day: it is irresponsible to visit one litter of unvaccinated puppies after another in this manner as you just cannot take the risk that you might carry infection with you.

Choosing an Adult

It is obviously easier to choose a show dog with certainty if you can purchase an adult. Then you can really see what you are getting, rather than buying what someone once described as 'a hope and a dream'. However, such a purchase is likely to be very expensive, as the breeder will seek recompense for perhaps a year or more of careful and knowledgeable rearing. Also, one would regard with a certain suspicion anyone who suddenly offered for sale a young adult Shih Tzu as a certain winner – if it's that good, why aren't they keeping it themselves? None the less, it does occasionally happen that a really good show prospect comes onto the market, and such an opportunity is worth taking.

Occasionally, a breeder may decide to part with a really promising young bitch – perhaps because there are just too many dogs at home already – and offer the youngster on what is called 'breeding terms'.

This means that the bitch, and it is invariably a bitch, is purchased at a reduced price, and that the buyer then contracts to mate her at an agreed time to the stud dog of the seller's choice, and thereafter for the seller to come and take his own choice from the resulting litter. After this, the bitch may belong to the purchaser, although up to the arrival of the puppies she may have been owned jointly. The arrangements can vary, but this is the sort of thing generally meant by breeding terms. I can only tell you that I have heard of so many such arrangements ending in tears that I always advise against them. Imagine how you would feel, having had all the work, worry and expense of breeding a litter, to see the pick of the puppies (or maybe the best two from the litter, depending on the terms) taken away from you. It must be admitted, however, that if this is the only way that you can afford a bitch of quality, than breeding terms should not be ruled out. Much will depend on the relationship between the two parties to the agreement. Certainly it is important to have every possible detail in writing, including what is to happen if the bitch proves infertile, and any other contingency that you can think of.

Someone looking for a pet may also be attracted by the idea of getting an older puppy or young adult, perhaps thinking that it would be advantageous to have a dog that is already house-trained. In reality, however, it doesn't always work like that, because successful house-training in one home may not transfer to another. A friend of mine recently took back for retraining a Shih Tzu that she had bred, because his owner of nearly a year had failed to get the house-training sorted out; back in his breeder's home, the dog behaved impeccably, with no mistakes. This, however, was an extreme example, and most Shih Tzus are remarkable for their great adaptability at any age.

When it comes to choosing a pet, there are sometimes good reasons for considering an older Shih Tzu. An elderly person might not feel able to cope with all the traumas of house-training and long walks, but would welcome the companionship of a slightly more placid and sedentary animal. In these cases, it is well worth considering a rescue dog: any one of the rescue organizations that specialize in caring for Shih Tzus will be happy to discuss your needs. Good rescue co-ordinators take great pride in matching up the right dog with the right owner, and you will have the reward of giving a good home to an especially deserving dog.

It can happen that a dog in need of rescue is also a problem dog, usually on account of his past experiences, and there is always a need for very special people with the patience to take these on. I can best

Lottie was rescued by the Southern Shih Tzu Rescue and is now happily settled in a loving home. (Photo: A. C. Marsh.)

illustrate this by describing one particular case. 'Lottie' was found by a dog warden. It was obvious that she had recently had puppies but, despite searching for them all over, he could not find them. She was malnourished, with a matted coat, and one eye had a perforated lens. A vet said she must have been in agony. There was also some injury to her liver, possibly caused by a kick. The Southern Shih Tzu Rescue took Lottie in hand and, after some expensive veterinary surgery, her eye was saved although not the sight. Despite her traumatic experiences she was, and still is, a lovely and affectionate little dog, and is very much loved by the family in Kent who gave her a caring and permanent home. The rescue organizations will discuss this sort of situation with anyone who feels they could cope with a dog in special need, but this is not the sort of responsibility that should be taken on lightly.

4

Puppy Care
and Development

The first year of a dog's life is of vital importance in determining his adult appearance, his health and strength, and even his temperament. You may not be able to make a silk purse out of a sow's ear, but I firmly believe that the opposite is possible and that lack of the right environmental factors can damage the development of any animal, no matter how good its genes may be. Time and effort spent in providing the right food, the most appropriate living conditions and the correct training will be well rewarded in the pride and joy you can take in the finished product, your Shih Tzu companion, be he a pet or show dog, or both.

Bringing a New Puppy Home

The day the young puppy leaves his mother and brothers and sisters will be the most traumatic in his life to date, so prepare in advance to make the experience as pleasant as possible. If a puppy has not travelled in a car before, he may cry or even be sick, so be prepared to clean up with paper towels if necessary. When you get home, take the puppy into the garden at once and remain there until he has relieved himself, at which point be very voluble in giving praise: this is the very first step in house-training, and it helps if you get it right.

On that first day do not keep picking the puppy up and fussing over him, but let him explore his new surroundings in his own way. He will be ready to come to you for a cuddle soon enough. There need to be rules for the human members of the family too, one of which should be that when the puppy goes to sleep he is allowed to do so and is left in peace. He will be awake again and ready to play in his own time.

It is vital to have decided exactly where the new puppy is to spend the night and to keep to this rigidly. The first night the new arrival will miss his mother and litter-mates, so is very likely to cry. It is far too easy in this case to gather him up into your arms and take him to your bed, thereby establishing a precedent that any intelligent Shih Tzu puppy will quickly latch on to and exploit to the hilt. Be firm, for the crying will last only for a while and not all night. It is a good idea to try leaving a radio on quietly in the background in the kitchen or wherever the puppy's bed is, or else a loudly ticking clock for company.

The breeder will have provided a diet sheet, and probably some suitable food for the first day or so, to avoid any danger of tummy upsets being caused by a change of diet. Do not be alarmed if your puppy is too excited or confused to eat much at first. This is only the first day, and correct management, with a generous helping of patience and love, will soon settle the new member of the family into a happy and healthy routine. Above all, try not to change the diet, at least at first, as the new member of your household has quite enough to contend with (and so do you) without a bout of diarrhoea into the bargain.

If the new puppy is being brought into a house where other dogs live, take care to avoid jealousy from the older canine residents. Make sure that the latter get a great deal of fuss and love, and always greet them before the youngster. Do not leave the newcomer alone with the other dog or dogs until you are sure that he has been accepted, and try to interfere as little as possible when an older dog disciplines the younger. This is bound to happen, and so long as the puppy shows a respectful demeanour towards his elders there will be no trouble. In the wild a pack of dogs or wolves will have a distinct pecking order, and so it will be with a group of domestic dogs – or even with just two. This is something they will work out better for themselves with the minimum of intervention from you. The relationships between dogs are remarkably complex, and the arrival of a new dog sometimes seems to cause a bit of friction between the existing members of a group for a day or two, but they all settle down quite soon.

Three to Six Months

First Grooming Steps

Early grooming is mainly concerned with getting the puppy used to being handled, which he should accept as an enjoyable experience. As with so much else about puppy rearing, it is wise to start as you mean to go on. An ideal, which I have rarely if ever managed to attain, is to establish a routine, with grooming taking place at the same time each day and in the same place. Some owners prefer to groom their Shih Tzu on a table, others like to have the dog on their laps. The latter is possibly an easier option with a young puppy. Brush and comb very gently indeed, talking quietly and reassuringly as you go, and do not at first persist beyond the limits of the puppy's patience. This grooming time, quiet and free from distractions, can become a mutual pleasure for dog and owner, with the dog so relaxed he may even go to sleep; alternatively it can become a battle, with the Shih Tzu objecting every step of the way, and the owner feeling stressed about the whole thing. Do not let the latter situation develop, but exercise the utmost patience and take things step by step. For example, if at first your puppy does not like to lie on his back to have his tummy groomed, leave that until another day rather than letting a battle of wills develop – those are battles that a Shih Tzu is, by its very nature, likely to win!

Grooming of the head and face needs to be carried out daily without fail, even from this early stage. Check that the eyes are clear and shiny, with no discharge, and that there is no damage to the surface of the eyeball. Inspect the ears, too, for any signs of discharge, and also for any odour – one of the early signs of trouble may be a slightly nasty smell from within the ear. Inspect the teeth daily, to get your dog used to this procedure. Next comes the washing of the whiskers, not with lashings of soap and water at this early stage but just by wiping a moist cotton pad gently around the mouth area.

Vaccination

When puppies are born, they receive immunity against disease through ingesting the first milk from their mother. This milk, called the colostrum, will give them protection through the early weeks of their life until they reach the age when it is appropriate to have them vaccinated. Consult your vet about when exactly to have this done, but it should be around twelve weeks of age. This first vaccination will consist of a package, protecting against distemper, infectious canine hepatitis, leptospirosis and parvovirus; it is only after the vaccination programme is completed that the puppies may be taken out into the wider world. Further doses of vaccine will be required, and it is recommended that annual boosters are given throughout the dog's life.

Diet

Newly weaned puppies from about eight weeks old will take two feeds of milk and two of meat per day (*see* Chapter 10). As the amount taken at each meal increases, a puppy can be fed three times daily instead of four. I have often found that they do this of their own accord, usually by rejecting milk feeds by the time they are four months old. Whether you are rearing a puppy you have bred yourself or one you have just brought home, the rules are the same as far as changes of diet are concerned: always make any changes gradually if you want to avoid the penalty of an upset tummy. The amount eaten at each meal varies greatly from puppy to puppy, as does the rate of growth. I would just advise making sure that there is always plenty: a Shih Tzu at this age is growing so fast that his needs are greater than those of many adult dogs. As a rough guide to progress, at four months a Shih Tzu will have reached about half his adult weight.

House-Training

The basics of house-training are laid when the young puppies go to the newspaper in the corner of their pen to urinate and defecate (*see* Chapter 10), but further progress is best made through individual attention to each pup, something much more easily achieved once the litter has been dispersed. Once you are dealing with one puppy, or at most two, whether you have bred them yourself or brought them in, the use of a puppy pen is no longer so necessary, although there must still be a pen or other enclosed area where the puppy may be confined for his own safety at times when the owner is not able to supervise. Leaving an unwatched puppy loose in the house can be a recipe for disaster, not so much for the damage he may do to your possessions as for the danger to his own life from chewing electric wires and so on. Although the Shih Tzu puppy at this age will not have much control over his bladder, you will notice that he is likely to urinate when waking up and after eating, so these are the times to take him into the garden, stay there together until he has relieved himself, praise him profusely and only then take him back in again.

Of course there will be accidents, each of which is going to be a set-back in the house-training process, but there is no point in shouting and punishing the puppy because he will have even less control over his bladder if he is thoroughly frightened. You may find that if you have newspapers laid at intervals through the house he will go to them, in which case the papers can be gradually moved towards the door preparatory to the moment of breakthrough when at last he goes to the door and asks to go out. The whole process depends on the owner dancing in constant attendance on the puppy, which is one of the reasons why so many breeders are unwilling to sell a puppy to a household where everyone is out at work all day, unless the buyers are willing and able to make adequate puppy-sitting arrangements.

'No'

Having a young puppy to rear takes up an enormous amount of time, something I conveniently tend to forget until the next one arrives. The hard work involved, the setbacks and the frustration when the puppy forgets the latest piece of training can all be very wearing for the owner, and there have been occasions when I have asked myself why on earth I am doing all this. The answer, of course, is there on the floor at my feet. Having just chewed up one corner of my favourite rug and tiddled on another, a cheeky puppy is gazing up at me with eyes that speak as clearly as words could, and the message is, 'Pick me up and give me a cuddle please – all the mischief I've been getting into for the past hour or so has made me very tired!'

By this time your puppy will recognize his name, and should come to you when you call; always praise this behaviour, but if he does not

Playing can be very tiring!

come turn and walk away – never chase after him, as this will be taken as another sort of game, and will not achieve anything. Other lessons can be learned whilst owner and pup are together in the garden, such as that it is not a good idea to bite human fingers, and that digging up flowers is disapproved of. Already he will learn the inflexions of his owner's voice, and changes in the tone of voice are far more effective than just shouting. One of the most common mistakes is to spoil a puppy at this stage: they are so enchanting, but can be wilful too, so rules must be made and enforced. Spending a lot of time with a puppy is important in the training process, another reason not to take on a young puppy if you are obliged to be out of the house for a large part of the day.

Physical chastisement is not a suitable way of dealing with a naughty puppy in my view. When someone recently told me that she never slapped her puppy, preferring to bang a rolled up newspaper hard on the floor just behind him to startle him, I couldn't help thinking that this might have been counter-productive. It could surely have made the puppy nervous, or alternatively led him to attack newspapers, depending on his temperament.

In the case of my chewed rug, I simply said 'No,' in a firm voice with a downward cadence, lifted the puppy away from the activity, and distracted her by playing with one of her toys. When she returned to the corner of my rug I repeated this procedure, until finally just the word 'no' was sufficient to stop her. Had I come back into the room to find that the rug had been chewed in my absence there would, of course, have been no point in taking any action at all. You have to catch the puppy in the act to have any chance of curbing such behaviour. One of my friends once returned to a puppy who had been left alone for an hour or so to find that most of the wallpaper up to a height of about eighteen inches from the floor had been stripped from the wall and torn into shreds: I know my friend now has a puppy pen in which to leave her puppies when she has to go out, and is the first to admit that this gives her much more peace of mind as well as being less costly!

Lead Training

Together with his litter-mates, the Shih Tzu puppy will have had exercise in plenty, playing and running to and fro, but once he is on his own, approaching about four months of age and fully vaccinated, he can be taken out for walks. Do not overdo it at first, however willing the puppy may be, but instead let him exercise freely in the garden where he can stop and rest at will. Too much exercise is as harmful as too little for a young puppy, so common sense must be used to get the balance right by very gradually increasing the amount of exercise as he grows and develops muscle strength.

During all this play and exercise in the garden the puppy will be as happy to follow at your heels as to go off and explore or play alone – perhaps more so, since the owner is now taking the place of his litter-mates. Indeed, we have a joke at home about my 'puppy shuffle': this is a curious mode of locomotion which involves walking about without taking my feet off the ground, and which I adopt when a young puppy is around the house to avoid treading on him. But put a lead on him and wham! – on go the brakes. Putting on a very light collar without a lead attached is a useful first step; at first the puppy will try to get it off, but he will soon learn to accept it and ignore its presence. Next, attach a lead, but do not on any account drag him along at this point, rather let him lead you. I have found that lead training proceeds more successfully if I take the puppy out of the garden and into the street in front of the house for the first lessons, as in these unfamiliar surroundings he is more likely to follow at my side for security. Sometimes I have found it effective to take along an adult dog for company and to give the puppy confidence, but you have to be careful not to let him become dependent on the older dog. Without pulling on the lead, encourage your puppy to follow you by calling his name. Praise him when he does. If he doesn't, give a short, quick tug on the lead to remind him you are at the end of it and call him again. The time taken to train a Shih Tzu to walk on the lead varies quite a lot from one puppy to another, but it does not usually take too long, and some breeders advise starting much earlier than I have suggested, even at six weeks.

Socialization

A young Shih Tzu has made a good start on the road to being socialized if he has learned to play with his owner, to be handled by all the members of the family as well as by visitors, to relax and accept regular grooming, and to interact with any other dogs in the household. Most of this learning has taken place within the familiar and secure home environment, however. Equally important is to socialize him in public, to take him for rides in the car, to visit other people in their homes, and to meet strange dogs. As soon as the course of vaccination is complete, it is time to start familiarizing a puppy with the outside world.

Do not take a baby puppy straight into the centre of a busy town for his first outing. Begin with a stroll in a quiet street and then, as he becomes used to the traffic, build up to busier ones. A walk through a pedestrian precinct (if dogs are allowed) can help the puppy to get used to strangers, and as Shih Tzu puppies are so pretty you will find that lots of people want to stop in order to talk to him and stroke him. All of this is good socialization.

Training for the show ring will be dealt with in Chapter 7, but I must mention ringcraft classes here, because they are very useful for socializing your puppy, even if you have no intention at all of actually showing your Shih Tzu. Ringcraft classes can be found in any area in Britain, and are run by the various local canine societies, whereas socialization classes as such are not always so easily found. I am lucky in having some local classes which are run exclusively for small breeds of dog. A great feature of these is the 'interval', during which the doors are securely closed, the owners take tea together and the dogs and puppies are let off their leads and allowed to get to know each other and play together. On their first visit, puppies sometimes retreat under a chair to watch the dogs cavorting about the hall, but they cannot resist all the fun for long and soon come out and join in.

Six Months to a Year

This is the final phase of puppyhood, during which the Shih Tzu completes most of his physical growth and consolidates all the good behaviour he has learned. By now his second teeth should be through, although Shih Tzus are sometimes a bit slow to get these. They may take a month or more to complete their dentition, and often suffer discomfort whilst teething, rubbing their jaws along the floor and sometimes going off their food for a time. This is an anxious time for the owner who has ambitions to show the puppy, as incomplete dentition can be a disadvantage in the ring, as can a jaw which becomes too undershot, or a wry mouth.

Apart from imperfect teeth and faults in jaw placement, neither of which is going to improve, there are other developments in the potential show dog which can seem discouraging, but which often come right again later. One such is the topline, which may rise towards the rear at some stages of growth; this characteristic is more common in some lines than in others, and seems to happen when the Shih Tzu's forequarters grow at a different rate from the hindquarters. The good news is that this will very often right itself as the dog matures. Tail carriage can also change, particularly during teething, but this too may well return to what it was before. It is not unusual for a puppy still to be slightly loose in front at seven or eight months, especially if he is of the heavy boned type; this must not be confused with the fault of being out at elbow, which is not going to improve. A loose front will tighten as the muscles strengthen, especially with the aid of controlled exercise. Walking the puppy uphill on a hard surface and at a steady pace can do wonders for a loose front.

Because a Shih Tzu puppy may appear gawky and rather plain during certain stages of growth, it is a good thing to keep firmly in mind the quality you saw in your pick of litter at eight weeks and which caused you to choose this pup for show. There is always the hope that as he grows up all will come right again. That said, it will not do to delude yourself if he has deveoped a bad fault, one which is not going to improve. Common sense and the Breed Standard must always be your guide. It is only when a Shih Tzu is one year old that you can really begin to assess his quality for sure, which is why some dogs do so very well in the show ring as puppies but never really hit the high spots again once they become adults.

From six months onwards, when he may be expected to weigh about two-thirds of his final adult weight, a puppy will do very well with two meals each day, although his food still needs to be high in protein compared with the maintenance diet suitable for an adult dog. Special foods are made to meet a dog's needs during the growing phases, and these have been used very successfully by Shih Tzu owners. It goes without saying that a growing puppy must never be kept short of food or allowed to become thin, yet people sometimes forget that the opposite condition can be equally harmful. Actually, it is much easier to take the weight off a greedy, fat dog than it is to get weight on a fussy eater. To achieve the former, simply cut out all tit-bits between meals, reduce the calorie content of the food whilst retaining the protein content, and make sure the puppy is having plenty of activity. To encourage a poor eater is always harder I find, although I shall offer some suggestions in Chapter 5.

Training should have produced a six-month-old puppy who will come when you call his name, who will walk at your side without pulling and who is clean in the house. He should further have learned the basic niceties of what is and what is not acceptable, so that he will not chew the furniture, bite his owner or jump up at people when they visit. At least, that is the theory. Shih Tzus do not as a rule bark incessantly, but should be taught to be quiet on command. Whether you choose to go in for further formal training is very much a matter of personal choice.

I have seen a group of Shih Tzus having great fun with an agility course; if you like the idea of agility training you will need to find a class that provides a mini-agility course. A friend of mine took her Shih Tzu to agility classes for a time: although the bitch soon knew well enough what was required, a high standard of achievement was never reached because she preferred to improvise variations on the exercises instead, and shamelessly played to the gallery until the owners of the bigger and more obedient dogs were convulsed with laughter at her antics. One of the agility exercises consisted of a see-saw: the dogs had to walk up one end and then pause to tip the further side down with their own weight before walking down and off the end of the plank. Tamsey quickly mastered the theory of this with typical Shih Tzu intelligence, but soon developed her own technique: at the pivoting point of the see-saw she would lie down and then, as the plank tilted under her weight, she would slide down it on her tummy, one paw trailing elegantly over the edge.

Another training option is to go to obedience classes. Who knows, you may succeed in making me eat my words on the subject of Shih Tzus and obedience (*see* Chapter 3).

From the age of six months, a puppy may be taken to shows, and this is something the prospective exhibitor looks forward to keenly. But do not be in too much of a hurry to rush a youngster into the show ring, particularly if he is patently a slow developer. Every puppy should be allowed to enjoy puppyhood, and every owner should be happy to enjoy it too. All too soon the puppy is grown up and you will be looking back on the photographs of that fluffy bundle of fun and mischief and wondering where the years have gone.

5

Adult Management

Feeding

When I was a little girl, living in a largely farming community, no one ever actually bought dog food. All the dogs in the village lived on kitchen scraps and offcuts from our friendly butcher, and very well they did too. In contrast, almost everyone I know today buys dog food of one sort or another, be it tinned, frozen or dried. There is a bewildering variety of commercial dog food available.

Many people are quite happy to use one of the complete dried foods, which are formulated to provide perfectly balanced nutrition in every meal. Their dogs seem to thrive, although eating in this way can hardly be described as natural. A wild animal's natural feeding pattern is more likely to consist of periods of glut and famine, and its food rarely turns up in balanced portions.

For those who are interested in feeding a dog in a much more natural way, I cannot do better than recommend Ian Billinghurst's book on this subject (*see* Further Reading). Dr Billinghurst is a practising vet in Australia, and writes a fascinating exposition of the principles and practice of natural feeding without recourse to commercial dog foods. One of the most telling points he makes about the latter is that the manufacturers design them to appeal to the human eye and sense of smell, since it is people and not dogs who buy such products. A commercial dog food also has to be highly palatable to ensure a dog eats it readily, even if this involves making it tasty with such additives as sweeteners. I do not follow the dietary regime advocated by Dr Billinghurst to the letter, not least because some of the foods he recommends are hard to obtain if you live in a town, but I do try to include as many of his suggestions as is practicable. Above all, the advantage of reading his book is that it opens one's mind to all the possibilities.

Although the dog is a carnivorous animal, this does not mean that he needs an all-meat diet and nothing else. Dogs fed solely on meat are more prone to skin problems than others. At the other extreme I have met owners who insist that their dogs absolutely adore a vegetarian diet, but I cannot help suspecting that these are people who are inflicting their own preferences on their pets. Within these two extremes, the Shih Tzu seems to thrive on a wide range of diets. My own preferred regime is to feed about half of the dog's diet as meat, ringing the changes between lamb, tripe and chicken for choice, with the remainder of the diet consisting of cereal in the form of cooked brown rice, vegetables, and a supplement to provide the necessary vitamins and minerals in the correct proportions. My adult dogs also have biscuits as treats, and enjoy steamed fish or the occasional boiled egg as a change. Pasta has always been a favourite with all my Shih Tzus. I also give milk to those who like it.

When it comes to buying food for a dog, the cheaper foods often provide just the bare minimum of required nutrients. You get what you pay for, and it is wise always to buy the very best you can afford. There are one or two commonsense rules to observe, whatever you choose to feed to your Shih Tzu. When feeding tinned food, always read the instructions carefully, to determine whether the tin contains a 'complete' food or if it is meat-based and therefore requires the addition of some form of cereal. When you use one of the dried foods, it is essential to make sure that the dog always has a plentiful supply of fresh drinking water. This is even more important if the food is one of those which is fed dry rather than being reconstituted with liquid. Hygiene should also be regarded as vital: feeding bowls must be kept scrupulously clean, and you should dispose of any uneaten food after about half an hour.

Commercial dog foods normally carry advice about the recommended daily intake for dogs according to their weight. However, it has been my experience that individual Shih Tzus vary in the amount of food they need, and it is a matter of trial and error to decide what is suitable for each dog. This changes at different stages in the life cycle, with an old dog needing less food than he did when in his prime. When several dogs are kept together, mealtimes should be supervised closely, for a greedy Shih Tzu will be happy to gobble his own ration and then steal someone else's, particularly if he is the dominant dog in the pack.

A Shih Tzu at twelve months of age will be eating two meals each day. Some people like to continue with two meals into the dog's adult life, while others choose to feed only once a day. The decision can depend on your own lifestyle as much as anything else. I choose to feed my Shih Tzus one main meal each day, although they do have biscuits at breakfast time and for supper. Because routine is useful when keeping dogs, always try to feed at the same time each day. This will encourage a healthy appetite because the dog will look forward to mealtimes.

It may seem an indelicate suggestion to the novice dog owner, but one of the simplest ways to check that your Shih Tzu's diet is satisfactory is to keep an eye on what is coming out at the other end. Loose and runny stools suggest that the diet needs adjusting, as do excessively large or hard stools.

Obesity

Snacking between meals causes weight problems for dogs just as much as for their owners, and is the most common cause of obesity. My vet once said sadly of a very fat Shih Tzu, 'They're killing her with kindness,' and he repeatedly warned the owners about their bitch's weight problem, all to no avail. Obesity makes a dog less keen to take exercise, and the less active he is the fatter he becomes. A vicious circle is set up until the poor creature's health is seriously affected, to the extent of aggravating any heart condition or other health problems in later life as well as probably putting excessive strain on the dog's joints.

An overweight Shih Tzu should never be starved, not should he be exercised to an extreme degree, but instead a serious and long-term strategy should be implemented to reduce the weight gradually. Your vet will give advice, and may recommend a specially formulated diet food. But the simple fact is that prevention is not only better than cure, it is also very much easier. All Shih Tzu owners should resolve to keep a watchful eye on their dog's weight just as they do on every other aspect of the animal's well-being. People often ask how to decide just when their dog is overweight, to which the answer is to check for ribs: if when passing your hands down each side of the dog's flanks you are unable to detect the presence of ribs, instead just feeling a tubular body of flesh, then you have an overweight Shih Tzu.

The Thin Dog

At the opposite end of the scale from the overweight Shih Tzu is the one that will not put on weight, one that is just what we call a 'poor doer'. One of my favourite vets always disagreed with me about what constituted 'thin', often saying that the dog about which I was concerned was actually in excellent condition. From him I learned that a healthy dog is not a plump one, although some amongst the show fraternity continue to confuse 'well-bodied' with 'fat'. That said, there are none the less occasions when one comes across a dog that really does need to carry more weight.

One of the first and most obvious things to check, when dealing with a Shih Tzu that is underweight despite eating normally, is that he has been wormed regularly: there is nothing worse than the presence of worms for keeping any dog thin. Next should come a visit to the vet, to make sure that the weight loss is not caused by a condition such as diabetes. If there is no health problem, the solution is often to increase the food intake, and at the same time to feed a diet with a high calorific value.

More difficult to deal with is the reluctant eater. In all the many conversations I have had over the years on this subject, I have detected one common thread, namely that if the dog's regular eating pattern is disrupted then the anxiety of the owner only exacerbates the situation. The more a distraught owner tries to tempt and coax with food, the less likely it is that the Shih Tzu will settle down to eating regularly. It is another vicious circle.

You should try not to a fuss about a dog's eating habits, but you can still take steps to improve them, as I found out when I owned a bitch who came from a line of notoriously poor eaters and who ate irregularly at best. A course of Vitamin B12, which is supposed to stimulate the appetite, had no effect. Because I had not experienced the problem in such an extreme form before, I found it impossible to avoid feelings of panic as she grew more and more anorexic. Eventually I decided that she must be persuaded to eat, no matter what the food was, so I broke all the rules and tried titbit after titbit until I found a few items of food which seemed more palatable to her. I then tried different times of the day and different situations until I eventually discovered that she preferred eating small meals away from the competition of the others. Once we had established an eating pattern, eccentric though it was, I was able very gradually to increase the amounts until she was at last of a reasonable weight. I can tell you this was not easy: she was six years old before I was reasonably satisfied with her weight, and even in old age she was certainly never anywhere near to what could be called fat.

Most commonly, a difficult or finicky eater is one that lives without the company of other dogs, although as the above story shows this is not always the case. If you suspect that your Shih Tzu needs the competition of another dog to encourage him to eat, borrow another dog to see if feeding them together will improve matters, remembering to be careful lest jealousy on the part of either dog should lead to a disagreement.

Last, but by no means least, a male dog that is kept in company with one or more bitches is very likely to go off his food when there is a bitch in season around. Fortunately this will be only a temporary problem, but it is amazing how quickly body condition is lost. This can be a great cause of worry to the owner who wishes to exhibit such a male at a show, because the dog may be penalized for lack of condition. The only thing to do is to try to tempt him with his favourite delicacies and, if he can be persuaded to eat while he in pining for love, be sure to feed him the best quality food, high in protein.

Housing

The history of this breed shows that the Shih Tzu was developed as a dog to live in human company, so it seems ironic that it was probably not until it came to the West, and especially to Britain, 'the home of dog lovers', that it encountered the kennel and the cage. Neither of these is suitable as a permanent home for a Shih Tzu; deprived of companionship and stimulation, he will never develop his full potential, nor show the delightful aspects of his personality unless these are nurtured by human companionship. However, I do accept that there are occasions when a dog is best confined, the chief of which is when travelling by car. For all car journeys I would advise buying a travelling box or crate from the outset, because a dog of any age is much safer travelling that way, particularly if the crate is securely anchored within the car. If the car stops suddenly the dog will not be thrown across it, nor will he be hurled through the windscreen in the event of a crash, as happened to one Shih Tzu in the past. A dog that is secured in a crate will also be unable to escape onto a busy road, when he would endanger himself and others.

Young puppies are at risk if they are left unattended in an area where there are hazards such as electric wires that may be chewed. In fact, almost anything is liable to be chewed by a puppy, sometimes with ghastly results. I heard only recently of a Shih Tzu puppy that chewed enthusiastically on the skirting board in the owner's absence, with the result that a nasty sliver of wood lodged at the back of the pup's mouth and had to be cut free. To prevent accidents like this, it may be safer to confine a young puppy when you are not able to be with him, at least until he has learned what is and what is not edible! A puppy pen should be large enough to allow the puppy to play freely, and secured so that there is no danger of it collapsing onto its occupant.

Those of us who are unwise enough to keep together Shih Tzu dogs and bitches find that there are occasions when we need to separate the sexes, and pens can be useful for this too. I have found that the dogs accept this segregation more equably if it is part of the routine rather than something which occurs only when a bitch is in season, and so I have always made it a practice to provide separate sleeping quarters for the dogs and the bitches.

Just as a Shih Tzu will happily share your home and your daily life, he will also be more than willing to share your bed, but this is not always a good idea. Maybe you are happy to have just one dog on the bed, but what about two or three? It seems sad that a dog that has spent most of his life sharing his owner's bed sometimes has to be banished in old age because of some such problem as incontinence, so consider all the ramifications before making a decision. I guess that the majority of Shih Tzus make their beds on the sofa in the living room or have their own little beds in the kitchen or any other room in the house. Straw is not suitable as bedding, since it gets entangled in the long hair, as does sawdust, and newspaper will make the hair dirty. A dog duvet is ideal, one which is easily laundered and which fits cosily into a dog bed of a suitable size. These are easy to make by cutting a single-bed duvet into three sections, seaming the sides and then covering each with removable and washable covers designed along the lines of a pillowcase. You can even make the covers colour co-ordinated with the rest of your soft furnishings. Two or more Shih Tzus may elect to share a bed, just as they often sleep in a heap on the chairs, but I like to provide each of my dogs with a separate bed, a place he can regard as his very own, and have noticed that if a dog is unwell or tired he will invariably retreat to his own bed, where he will be left alone by the rest of the pack.

Exercise

Exercise is one of the key factors that contribute to a happy and healthy life for a Shih Tzu, but it is only one. Other activities include play, in which the owner must take part (especially if only one dog is kept), and plenty of mental stimulation to develop the dog's intelligence.

A healthy adult Shih Tzu will enjoy several walks a day, if you can manage this, and will often surprise his owner with his stamina. Finding a pace which is equally acceptable to dog and owner is highly desirable, as there is nothing less enjoyable than a walk during which one or the other is always lagging behind. Finding the right leash is essential. My Shih Tzus do not wear collars in the house, in order to preserve the coat around their necks, so I prefer a lead and collar combined into one. The lead needs to be very secure, so that the dog cannot escape by backing out, but should not be a check-chain, which is also bad for the coat. There are a huge variety available for sale in pet shops and at shows, so it is a matter of trial and error to find the very best one for the job. Responsible dog owners do not need to be reminded to 'pick up' after their dogs when walking them in the street.

One of the major problems with Shih Tzus in full coat is that they tend to return from walks with an amazing amount of debris caught up in their hair – everything from leaves and burrs to quite large twigs. If this collection is left in the coat for any length of time it will soon cause tangling, so the wisest course is to check through the coat and clear any detritus as soon as the walk is over.

On a rainy day even a short walk will result in an extremely wet Shih Tzu, not only because these dogs are so heavily coated but also because they are short-legged. The easiest way to deal with a soaked dog is to wrap him in a large dry towel: do not on any account rub as this will tend to snarl up the coat, but just pat and gently squeeze the towel round the body and feet. What was a damp, bedraggled little animal will soon be dry again, as the coat is usually only damp on the surface. The exception to this is when there is snow on the ground. Shih Tzus love to romp in the snow, but the snag is that they soon get balls of it gathered into the hair of their legs and stomach. Never try to pull or comb the snow out of the coat, but stand the dog in a bowl of warm water: the snow will melt away in moments, and then you just have a wet dog to deal with. Some pet shops sell waterproof coats which cover the body and legs of the dog; the coat must fit well if the dog is to walk freely and happily while wearing it.

Pet shops are also a source of lots of different toys, and it is often the least expensive that provide the most lasting pleasure. Avoid toys that have a squeak or whistle which the Shih Tzu might be able get

Ch. Santosha Royal Flush enjoying himself in the garden. Note his level topline. (Photo: Jean Luc.)

out and swallow, those that are made of brittle plastic which might shatter, and those that are so small they could be swallowed. A ball provides endless fun, but should be of such a size that it could not possibly be swallowed or get stuck in the throat.

If you have a garden you will find that your Shih Tzu will get quite a lot of exercise by running around, just exploring or chasing a ball. This is a breed that is inclined to be 'into everything', rather like a small child, so the garden must be prepared for Shih Tzu occupancy. First make sure that it is escape-proof, and secondly ensure that there are no poisonous plants within reach. Get rid of any plants that have spikes or thorns. I have never had any rose bushes in my garden since, many years ago, one of my puppies rushed into a bush and punctured his eye on one of the thorns: it was an horrific injury and we were lucky that he did not lose the eye. If you must have roses, choose standards.

Daily Grooming

Coat care is dealt with in detail in Chapter 6, but there are other aspects of grooming that must be attended to, and on a daily basis.

Ch. Snaefell Limited Edition at an outdoor show.

It doesn't take more than a few minutes to attend to the dog's face each day, preferably after feeding, and your Shih Tzu will get used to this routine and come to expect it.

First, gently comb away any fragments of food from the whiskers, and then wash the whiskers and beard if necessary, as it so often is. If the beard and whiskers are white, you must take special measures to maintain their pristine appearance. Preparations devised for just this purpose are available at pet shops and at shows; most have the added advantage that they are safe to use on the dog's face, where you are

A fine-toothed comb is the best tool for cleaning food from the whiskers.

working in such close proximity to the eyes. White whiskers stay whiter if you dry them thoroughly after washing them; in any case, if you do not do this the average Shih Tzu is likely to try to dry his own whiskers, usually by the time-honoured method of rubbing his face along the side of the furniture or, even worse, on the stones of the patio. Either of these activities will render the Shih Tzu face whiskerless in no time at all.

Check that the eyes are clear and free from discharge, and that no hair is touching the eyeball, then gently comb out any accumulated discharge from the coat at the inner corners of the eyes. A small-toothed comb will be required for this. Similarly, check inside the ears for discharge, wax or matted coat. Never poke down into the ear cavity, but if there is an accumulation of hair growing inside the ear this can be pulled out, a few hairs at a time. Take a cotton bud, moistened with olive oil, and clean the opening of the ear, but *do not* probe deep into the ear. Clean the teeth, for which purpose you can buy special dog-toothpaste, and look to see if the teeth are sound and free from a build-up of tartar. Lastly, comb through and re-tie the hair of the topknot if it needs doing, as it almost always does.

Once you have finished with the head, check the other end of the Shih Tzu. Faeces can get caught up in the long hair around the anus, and it can not only make the dog extremely uncomfortable and sore but may also prevent further defecation. This should not be a common occurrence if the diet is correct and the stools are firm. The quickest way to deal with dried-on faeces is to powder the dog's trousers liberally with talcum powder and then brush them clear; if the trousers are still dirty the answer will be to rinse the coat with warm water.

One more area of the Shih Tzu needs daily checking, or rather four areas: the feet. If the hair between the pads becomes matted this will cause the dog to go lame, and must in any case make walking extremely uncomfortable. To avoid matting trim away as much of this hair as you can. Use a pair of short-bladed, blunt-ended scissors, and be very careful not to snip the flesh of the pad. This delicate operation is best performed when the dog is relaxed; I find it easiest to accomplish whilst my Shih Tzu lies asleep on my lap.

While checking that the pads are clear of hair and free from cuts and abrasions, look at the nails too. The frequency with which these will require cutting depends partly on the surface on which the dog normally runs; I was surprised to find, when I moved from a house with a hard-tiled floor to one which was carpeted throughout, that the nails needed to be cut very much more often. The nails of an adult Shih Tzu are surprisingly tough, so the best tool to use is the guillotine type of clippers available from any pet shop. Each nail has nerves and blood vessels running down inside, in the part known as the 'quick'. Cutting into the quick must be avoided at all costs, since this will not only cause profuse bleeding but will also be painful for the dog. Any dog which has once had the quick of the nail caught by the clippers will be exceedingly reluctant to have his nails cut again! When the nail is pink it is comparatively easy to see the quick running through it and thus clip off the tip of the nail safely, but this is not easy when the nail is coloured black. To play safe, cut only a tiny piece off the nail at one time: little and often is the rule. If bleeding does occur it can be stemmed by applying either permanganate of potash or a styptic pencil.

Particular care must be taken to check the dew-claws where these are present on the Shih Tzu, since they are never worn down by walking. They will continue to grow on into a circle until they actually pierce the flesh unless they are trimmed regularly. It is because these dew-claws are such a potential nuisance that some breeders prefer to have them removed when the puppies are a few days old.

Care of the Older Dog

Looking back over many years of Shih Tzu ownership, I have noticed that the dogs have aged at different rates: one or two became quite staid in their behaviour by the time they were eight or nine years old, whilst others remained lively and active well into their teens. Rather than define old age in the Shih Tzu in terms of years therefore, I would prefer to describe it as the stage of life at which the dog becomes less active and more fixed in his behaviour, sleeping for longer periods and showing less interest in new experiences. Hearing and eyesight may begin to fail, the hair may become brittle and sparse, and as the joints become less supple a stiffness in the gait can be observed.

As your Shih Tzus age, they need and deserve an extra bit of tender loving care. This will involve making sure that they have somewhere to sleep that is warm and free from draughts, as well as ensuring that they have enough exercise to keep them fit without overtaxing their stamina. If an old dog is greedy and inclined to grow fat, his intake must be restricted a little, but the food given must be of good quality and will still need to include protein. Regular veterinary checks will detect the onset of any serious condition such as kidney failure or heart disease, as will the owner's vigilance. Bad teeth, the signs of which include a smell on the breath and continual rubbing of the face along the floor or the furniture, can cause a lot of discomfort and may prevent the dog from eating normally. Once decayed or loose teeth have been removed you will notice a rapid improvement.

Your Shih Tzu will still get around the home quite happily even if his vision and hearing become very much impaired, although he will feel much happier and more secure if you avoid moving the furniture about, and if you stick to the household routine. I once had a much loved Shih Tzu bitch who was completely blind and deaf, but this was not immediately evident to visitors because she toddled around so confidently in the surroundings with which she was familiar. She also demonstrated that there was nothing wrong with her sense of smell by descending with great enthusiasm on any dish of food in her vicinity. Eating and sleeping seemed to be that old lady's main sources of pleasure for the last year of her life, during which we were careful to ensure that she suffered no stress and that she was not in any pain.

One day any Shih Tzu owner may be faced with the difficult decision to end a pet's life, a decision which will save further suffering for the dog but which may come close to breaking the owner's heart. Rest assured that after the trauma of such an event there is comfort in the knowledge that it was the right decision to make, and that the vet helped the dog to die quite painlessly. With the passing of time our pet lives on in our memories of happier days, and those of us who have done any breeding are sometimes fortunate enough to see an echo of a past favourite in the mannerisms of his of her children or grandchildren. This can be a blessing indeed.

6

Coat Care and Presentation

Picture for a moment a Shih Tzu just returned from a walk on a damp November day. His coat is bulked out with leaves and twigs which became caught up when he ran beneath a tree, his feet are wet and black as a result of splashing through an oily puddle, his once-white whiskers are an unappealing mud colour, and his topknot hangs rakishly to one side because he had a good scratch whilst his owner's attention was diverted. And now imagine the same dog just ready to enter the show ring. His coat hangs immaculately to the floor from a dead straight centre parting with never a hair out of place, his whiskers and feet gleam white and pristine, and his topknot is perfectly arranged so as to complement his expression. These two images are enough to explain just why the Shih Tzu coat can be his crowning glory and the joy of his proud owner, or alternatively a source of frustration – or both at different times! Transforming the scruffy dog into the immaculate one requires a combination of

Penny Lane, co-owned by the author and Jan Borrett, prefers the scruffy look…
(Photo: David Borrett.)

dedication, application, routine, experience, technique and art, all attainable by anyone who is willing to learn and to persevere.

In order to grow a long, dense coat the Shih Tzu must carry the right genes for that characteristic just as for any other trait of physical appearance. Next, the dog must receive the right sort of nutrition from birth in order to fulfil his genetic potential. I have talked about nutrition generally in Chapter 5, but for the coat in particular I have found it very beneficial to give my adult Shih Tzus one teaspoonful per day of a sunflower-oil spread, which is rich in Vitamin E. Use of this over a period has always seemed to give my dog's coats an extra sheen as well as an added elasticity. Thirdly, the long coat must be given the correct care if it is to be preserved once it has grown. In this chapter it is the third of these requirements that I address, bearing in mind that there are no hard and fast rules about coat care and that the advice must always be adjusted to suit the individual coat.

A quick brush soon makes Penny Lane look tidy again. (Photo: David Borrett.)

Grooming Tools and Equipment

Table

Do not make the mistake of thinking that any old table will do. It must be stable, easy to clean, and with a non-slip surface so that the dog feels relaxed and confident in his footing, and it should be available in the same place each time grooming is to take place. Ideally, a Shih Tzu will be persuaded to lie on his side on the grooming table, to permit the grooming of his flanks and stomach. Never leave a dog unattended on a table, at a show or at home, lest he jumps off and hurts himself. For your own comfort, and to avoid getting a bad back, it is important to have the table at the right height. If you intend to show your Shih Tzu, you might invest in a special rubber-topped grooming table; these are sold at all the major championship shows, and some combine the function of a table with that of a trolley for carrying your equipment to and from a show venue. A grooming table is rather expensive but should prove a worthwhile investment and last for years. If you do not intend to show your dog, the purchase of a special grooming table is certainly not necessary. Instead, buy a good-sized rubber mat, such as one of those sold for use in cars, and place this on a table or other worktop that is of a suitable height. If you are thinking about using a kitchen worktop, remember that hairs will fly everywhere. We have our grooming table set up in a well-lit corner of the garage, and this works well except in the depths of a particularly cold winter.

Grooming Box

Although not essential, a box or tray to hold all the equipment for grooming is a great asset as it keeps all the tools tidy when they are not in use. Small toolboxes with a series of neat little compartments are handy and inexpensive for this purpose.

Brushes

It is said that all good things come in threes, and this is certainly true of my indispensable dog brushes. The one with which a puppy first becomes acquainted is my pure bristle brush: it is the smallest size available and the natural bristles are set in a pneumatic rubber cushion, so it does not hurt the most tender of puppy skins. As the dog

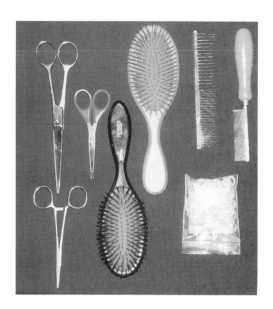

A selection of grooming tools.

grows up this brush will still be used, mainly on the whiskers and topknot. I have had my little bristle brush for years, and wouldn't be without it. As my Shih Tzus grow a longer and thicker coat I find that the pure bristle brush no longer penetrates deep enough, and so I progress to using a bristle and nylon brush, one which is constructed in the same way as the tiny brush but two sizes larger and with nylon bristles set among the natural ones. The final grooming brush consists of wire pins set in a pneumatic cushion, with the tip of each pin polished to a smooth, rounded point which will not scratch. This last brush is used to finish the coat at the end of grooming, drawing each hair into position with steady gentle strokes down each side of the dog. It also comes into service when I am making an initial attack on a large mat of coat prior to going in with a comb or scissors.

Using a brush requires a certain technique: draw it through the coat layer by layer, and carry each stroke smoothly down, right off the end of the hairs. If you use the brush jerkily, or with a flick at the end of each stroke, you are likely to snap the ends of the hairs. This breaking of the coat does not occur in a spectacular and immediately obvious fashion but takes place in tiny imperceptible increments, with the result that the effect is apparent only after the brush has been used incorrectly for a period of time.

Blunt-Tipped Knitting Needle

Although the long Shih Tzu coat falls naturally to either side of a parting down the centre of the back, this parting is not always perfectly straight. The knitting needle is a handy tool to straighten the parting: run the tip gently along the back of the dog, from the neck to the base of the tail.

Combs

Most grooming can be done with a general-purpose metal comb, one with coarse teeth at one end and fine teeth at the other. The only other comb which is useful is a very fine or 'flea' comb for cleaning the hair at the inner corners of the eye. Whereas a brush is used in long, steady strokes down the length of the hair, a comb must be used much more gently: work carefully through the coat to take out any dead or loose hair but stop the moment you encounter a knot.

Sprays and Conditioners

I do not like to brush the coat when it is dry, and find a fine-nozzled spray bottle containing plain water ideal for misting the hair before brushing. It is also useful when there is a lot of static in the coat.

There are so many spray products available, with more coming on the market all the time, that it would be foolhardy to recommend one more than another. In any case, the most suitable product very much depends on the type and texture of your Shih Tzu's coat, so choice is a matter of trial and error. There are 'anti-tangle' sprays available at most shows and at the larger pet shops, and these can be very helpful with a difficult coat. As a general rule, the more often a Shih Tzu coat is washed the greater the need for conditioners and sprays.

Topknot Bands

For tying up the topknot at a show, you will need special, very small elastic bands. Several of these will need to be used in order to build up the topknot of a heavily coated dog. Orthodontic elastics of a suitable size are sold at championship shows, or they can be bought by mail order from your breed club. These little bands should always be cut off very carefully, because any attempt to pull them off for re-use will inevitably result in loss of hair. At home, I like to use a more robust band for the topknot, such as the small elasticated bands that are used to fasten girls' ponytails, sold at high street chemists and some supermarkets. These can be carefully drawn off for re-use, and are easy to wash as well.

Scissors

For cutting out the hair between the pads of the feet, a pair of small, blunt-ended scissors will be needed. This is the only scissoring that should be needed for a breed that is traditionally not trimmed at all, but one glance around the show ring will reveal that these days owners are carrying out quite a bit of trimming in order to enhance the dog's appearance. Most owners are now trimming the hair round the base of each foot, which will give a tidy appearance and enable the dog to move smartly without tripping over sprawling foot furnishings. Other owners are obviously trimming along the bottom of the body hair. For the latter purposes, medium-weight trimming scissors made of stainless steel will be adequate. Scissors must always be kept clean and sharp, because nothing will spoil a dog's coat more than hacking at it with a blunt pair.

Nail Clippers

Except for tiny puppy nails, which can easily be trimmed with nail scissors, the guillotine type of nail cutters are easiest to use for a Shih Tzu. The nails can be surprisingly tough for such a small dog, and I have not found the clipper type of implement anywhere near so effective – in fact, these will sometimes crush the nail rather than cutting it cleanly.

Miscellaneous

Close by the side of my grooming table I keep a few extra items which always come in useful. There are tissues, or more economically a roll of toilet paper, which I use for mopping up spills, drying whiskers and a dozen other tasks, and there are small cotton-wool pads, which I find ideal for putting face cleaner on whiskers and moustaches. Petroleum jelly is another useful item as it can be smoothed on the hair around the eyes to prevent it from getting onto the eyeball and thereby causing irritation.

Brushing

Part of life with a Shih Tzu is giving the coat a thorough head-to-tail groom however often it is needed, be it only once a week for some types of coat or every other day for others. This will be in addition to the daily attention outlined in Chapter 5. Any new owner will soon be able to work out how often it is advisable to groom the coat, but extra vigilance is needed when the soft puppy coat is giving way to the adult. Generally this will happen when the puppy is ten or eleven months old. Grooming may well become a daily necessity then, for the hair will tend to mat and tangle really badly for a time. Fortunately this is only a temporary phase, so you just have to persevere until you find that grooming becomes much easier once again.

Always start by grooming the hair on the tummy, the chest and inside the legs: to do this you need to have your Shih Tzu lying on his side on the table, with his legs towards you. If the dog just will not cooperate you can have him lying tummy upwards in your lap with his head facing your chest. Failing this, the only other way to groom the chest and tummy is to sit the dog on the table facing you, holding him up into a begging position by the front paws; this is not an easy approach, since both hands are needed for some parts of the grooming, but you may have to try it as a last resort.

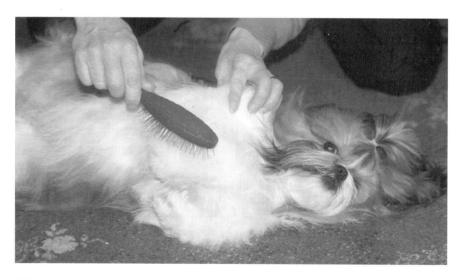

The best way to groom the hair on the tummy is to persuade the dog to lie on his side.

Do not wield the brush too vigorously, since the underpart of a dog is quite a sensitive area. Be sure to check where the legs meet the body – always a likely spot for knots. If you find a knot there, trim it away: even for a show dog this is not going to make any difference to the appearance. The hair round a male's penis can similarly be carefully trimmed away to help keep him clean and sweet-smelling. When you come across a knot elsewhere, first try to tease it apart with your fingers. Then take the comb and use the end with coarse teeth to tease out the tangle, working from the outside inwards and holding the hair between the knot and the body between your fingers so that you don't pull too hard and hurt the dog. If all else fails, a knot may have to be cut; should this be necessary, cut into the knotted hair away from the dog several times before gently using the comb to clear away the knot. Never cut across the coat as this will leave an obvious hole, whereas cutting down through the length of the coat will cause much less damage. The hair on the legs is more likely to tangle than anywhere else, especially if the dog has a very dense coat.

Once the hair on the tummy and legs is finished, flick all the body hair up and over the back before brushing it downwards again, a layer at a time, using the nylon and bristle brush. I like to spray each layer lightly with water or a coat dressing before brushing. At this stage the dog is still lying on his side. The purpose of working in layers like this is to get the brush right to the skin; if you stand the dog and brush the top of the coat, you can brush away all day without getting past the top layer. Use the comb only when it is necessary to take out a tangle. Once the first side is finished, turn the dog over so that he lies on his other side and repeat the process. I had one Shih Tzu who used to go to sleep whilst being groomed, and I clearly remember how he always looked quite indignant when I woke him up to turn him over. While you are going through the coat, layer by layer, look out for evidence of skin problems or external parasites (*see* Chapter 11).

When both sides of the body coat are thoroughly groomed and free of knots, stand the dog up, facing away from you, and straighten the parting down the centre of the back, using a comb or the tip of a blunt knitting-needle, before attending to the hair of the tail, round the backside and down the back of the legs. I find the hair on the tail to be the most fragile, and if I break off any hair this is where it most often happens. Finally, get the dog to sit facing you and groom the hair on the chest and neck, taking particular care to clear any knots behind and under the ears as there usually seems to be a knot or two here.

The parting along the centre of the back can be straightened with a comb or blunt-ended knitting needle.

All that remains to be groomed is the head and face. Here the fine-toothed end of the metal comb will be useful in getting out any tangles, but combing must be done very gently round the nose, eyes and mouth. This is the time to give the whiskers and beard an extra thorough wash, before you carry out the usual daily routine of attending to the eyes and ears, as described in Chapter 5. Part the whiskers in the centre of the top of the nose and then comb down to each side to form a frame for the muzzle.

From about five months of age the hair of the head above the nose is tied into a topknot; this keeps it out of the dog's eyes and food, and gives the face its distinctive appearance. That said, a badly placed

The hair on the chest and under the chin can be groomed whilst the dog is sitting facing you.

It is important to draw up just the right amount of hair for the topknot.

The hair of the topknot should not be pulled up too tightly.

topknot can quite ruin the expression, so it is worth practising until you can get it just right each time. Take the hair for the topknot from above the nose and eye, taking care not to draw up any beyond the outer corner of each eye nor from behind an imaginary line between the back of the ears. If the dog's head is small, take up less to make a narrower topknot. Be very careful, when placing a band on this bunch of hair, that it is not tied too tightly, as this can make the skin quite sore and will in any case cause the poor dog to scratch it all out again as fast as he can. If a Shih Tzu is very heavily coated you may need to use more than one band to hold the topknot in place, especially when getting ready to go into the show ring.

After a final settling of the body coat with the metal-pinned brush, there you have it – a beautifully groomed Shih Tzu, without a single tangle left in his coat. Doesn't he look fine? Enjoy the sight, because as soon as he is placed back on the floor the first thing he will do is to have a good shake. The time that the whole grooming process takes will vary according to the length and density of the coat. I have found that the dogs rather enjoy all the attention once they become used to the routine, and there is a certain amount of competitiveness amongst them as to who is the next to be groomed.

Side view of the selection of hair for the topknot.

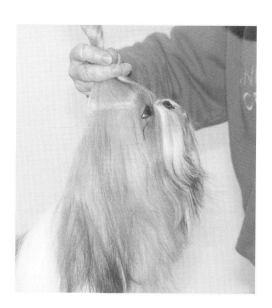

The finished topknot.

Bathing

One result of the modern emphasis on presentation for the show ring has been that show dogs are bathed more frequently than was ever dreamed of twenty years ago. Not only is the show dog bathed before every show, some are bathed weekly whether or not they are to be shown. What concerns me is that so much washing must surely take out many of the natural oils of the coat, with the result that more and more conditioning products have to be used to replace them. I prefer to bath even the show dogs as little as possible consistent with the requirements of showing. It is simpler to decide how often to bath pet dogs. The pet need be bathed only when he is dirty or smelly: in other words, make the decision largely on social grounds. I always make sure that the coat is free of all tangling before I bath any of my dogs, although other owners take a different view (*see* Extra Care for the Show Coat on page 99). Always gather together everything that is going to be needed before you start to wash a Shih Tzu.

The first bath for a puppy can be quite a traumatic experience, one I have always tried to delay until the baby is at least three months old. It is easier to bath a puppy in a bowl or even in the sink than in the bath. Make sure that the water is neither too hot nor too cold, and use a mild dog-shampoo, taking care that no soap gets into the eyes. Pour the water gently over the puppy from a jug, which will be much less alarming than a shower attachment or spray. After being washed, a puppy must be dried off completely before being allowed outside again.

An older dog can be washed in the bath using a shower attachment, but place a rubber mat in the bottom of the bath to provide a firm footing. The choice of shampoo and conditioner depends on the type of coat, but products that are marketed for human use are really not suitable and should be avoided. Someone who had used 'human' shampoo on her bitch's coat (because she had temporarily run out of her usual dog-shampoo), told me that the poor little creature began to scratch incessantly. Eventually the worried owner and her vet reached the conclusion that this incessant irritation was caused by the shampoo, which was discovered to be a brand that coated each hair and built up after each use. The problem was solved by using another product sold for use on human hair, namely a stripping shampoo designed to remove any build-up of other preparations. This cautionary tale reminds us all to be very careful when choosing a shampoo for dog washing. I would use washing-up liquid before I would use any shampoo about which I was not sure, and indeed have done just that on more than one occasion with no ill-effect. Shampoos and conditioners specifically manufactured for use on dogs are in plentiful supply, and most of them are excellent. In summer, it is a good idea to use an insecticidal shampoo.

Whatever shampoo is being used, I always prepare it, diluted according to the instructions and placed in a jug, before I fetch the dog to the bath. I prepare the conditioner beforehand as well. Several large towels are placed ready to hand, one of which I use to wrap around my waist like a sort of apron, to protect at least part of me from the splashes.

Once everything is ready, plug the dog's ears with cotton wool to keep out the water and settle him in the bath. First soak the coat thoroughly: this takes more time than many new owners imagine, as the long outer hairs are quite water-resistant. The shampoo should not be applied until the coat is really wet. Pour some of the shampoo down the parting of the back, and as it runs down each side work it into the hair with a squeezing movement of the fingers – do not rub or massage as this will tend to tangle the coat. Then pour a little shampoo onto each leg and foot in turn, and use the same technique to work up a lather before going on to wash the tail and rear end. I always lift my Shih Tzus up by the front legs to shampoo their tummies, and then

Soak the coat thoroughly before applying shampoo.

Int. Ch. Snaefell Little Flower, bred by Audrey Dadds and owned by Monique Colombe in France. (Photo: Jean Luc.)

Int., Can., Fr. & Lux. Ch. Hopei Lover's Du Domaine Des Atlantes must be the most widely travelled Shih Tzu to be pictured in this book. Bred by Annik Laurent in France, he was then campaigned to his title in Canada by Richard and Wendy Paquett before being imported from France to England by Christopher and Linda Ripley.

Ch. Firefox of Santosha, CC winner at Crufts in 1988 and 1991, was bred by Bert Easdon and owned by Sue and David Crossley. He was a grandson of Ch. Santosha Sunking. (Photo: Jean Luc)

Ch. Santosha Tiger Lily won the bitch CC at Crufts 1988, and then proceeded to beat her famous kennel-mate, Firefox, for Best of Breed. (Photo: Jean Luc.)

Ch. Grandavon Ming Toi.

Ch. Hashanah Take Me To The Top. (Photo: Mick Franks.)

Ch. Hashanah No Jacket Required. (Photo: Mick Franks.)

Ch. Santosha Chocolate Orange.
(Photo: David Crossley.)

Ch. Peekin Tashi-Tu. (Photo: Carol Ann Johnson.)

Ch. Santosha Red October. (Photo: David Crossley.)

Ch. Emrose Michelin Man. (Photo: David Dalton.)

Ch. Hashanah The Immaculate. (Photo: Mick Franks.)

Ch. Metadale Mungojerrie. (Photo: Brenda Heaton.)

Ch. Peekin Sophie-Tu. (Photo: Carol Ann Johnson.)

Ch. Huxlor Gino Ginelli. (Photo: Terese A'Len.)

Ch. Chelhama De Courcey. (Photo: Animals Unlimited.)

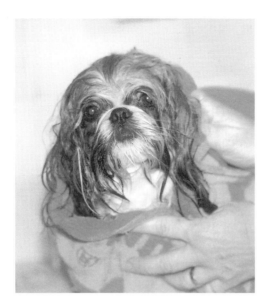

After bathing, remove excess water by wrapping the dog in a towel and gently squeezing the coat, but do not rub as this will cause tangles.

attend to the chest and head last of all. It is as their heads are washed that they seem to shake and shake, at which stage I find I get pretty wet myself.

Rinsing all the soap out of the coat is very important. At this stage, if the dog is very dirty, you may have to repeat the process all over again, and rinse once more. In any case, it is a good idea to give another, final rinse even after you think that all the soap is out. Application of a coat conditioner follows exactly the same pattern, and here again rinsing every bit out is essential. Then take a large towel and wrap the dog up to take out some of the water; soon the towel will be sopping, and must be replaced by another, so that when you come to dry your dog it is no longer dripping wet. Don't forget to remove the cotton plugs from the ears.

You can dry the Shih Tzu coat quite well with an ordinary domestic hair-dryer. I used just such a hand dryer for years, until I finally invested in a pedestal dryer that was specifically designed to do the job of drying a dog's coat. It was wonderful, one of the most useful things I have ever bought, and I would greatly recommend one to anyone intending to keep several Shih Tzus in full coat. A pedestal dryer is large and powerful enough to dry the coat in a fraction of the time, and leaves you with both hands free to attend to the dog. However these dryers are very expensive, and might seem exorbitantly so if you have just one Shih Tzu to care for.

In order to make the hair straight the Shih Tzu coat needs to be brushed while the dryer is being used to make the hair straight.

Finishing the completely dry coat with a comb.

A Shih Tzu's coat must be brushed all the time it is drying or else it will look curly and unkempt once it is fully dry. Just as with brushing, it is best to dry the hair in layers, and I know many owners who prefer to do this with their dogs on their laps because they find it very much easier than trying to do it on a table. Needless to say, if you choose this method you need yet another large towel, this time to keep yourself as dry as possible. The topknot should not be tied up until the hair on the head is completely dry.

Extra Care for the Show Coat

There are several myths about the care of a long coat for the show ring. One is that to preserve the coat on a show dog it is necessary to keep him confined and caged, or to wrap the coat or to oil it. Some show people do indeed keep their Shih Tzus in pens or cages, but they pay the penalty in loss of muscle tone in their dogs and do not deceive knowledgeable judges. The matching myth is that no dog can go on long walks, play and generally lead a normal doggy life, and at the same time keep a long, glamorous coat: on the contrary, this is possible but does require extra effort on the part of the owner, such as extra grooming and maybe a protective jacket for those November walks.

Putting oil into the coat can be helpful as a means of preserving it, and for this purpose coconut oil is considered particularly useful. If you do oil the coat, however, you must remove the oil completely before each show or else the coat may look limp and feel wrong. Oiling a Shih Tzu coat is something I have tried only a few times; I did not like the way it made the hair feel soft and of the wrong texture, nor did I enjoy having an oily dog sitting on my lap or the furniture. Some of the latest conditioning oils do not have this effect on the coat, so it is worth trying one if the coat seems to need it. Wrapping the coat in tissue paper protects it, but you lose the pleasure of seeing a dog in full coat rushing around the house with his hair flowing as he moves – a beautiful sight. I have never believed this can in any way be compensated for by any increase in the length of the coat.

Some exhibitors tell me that they never groom their Shih Tzus when just lightly sprayed, as described under Brushing on page 91, but only after they have bathed them. I cannot fault the results they obtain by this method, but find that it just doesn't work for me. The best advice I can give to new owners is that they should experiment and find out what suits them and their dogs' coats best.

A bad dog cannot be made a good one by clever hairdressing, but a good dog can appear less so if poorly presented. This is especially true when it comes to care of the topknot and whiskers, and here a little extra attention is required to get an attractive effect. The white whiskers on a parti-coloured dog must be really clean to look good, and this is most of all true of a black and white dog. One often sees a good black and white Shih Tzu in the ring, whose appearance is spoiled by the fact that the 'white' whiskers are in fact a grubby shade of grey or brown. The judge should not be influenced by this unduly, although if the decision for a placement is very close it may be just the sort of detail that becomes the deciding factor.

Keeping the whiskers white involves washing them at least once a day, and it may be necessary to use one of the special preparations for cleaning the face which are on sale at most of the big shows. Before these were marketed we all managed very well with home-made preparations. One favourite was a solution of boracic powder, a teaspoon to a pint of water; this was wiped into the whiskers, being careful to get none in the eyes, and then rinsed away. No matter what you use to wash the whiskers, the secret to keeping them white is above all to dry them immediately and always to keep them dry. In the old days we used to dry them by working in some fuller's earth or talcum powder, brushing this out and repeating until the hair was absolutely dry. If you do not dry the whiskers yourself, the Shih Tzu will dry himself by rubbing, and do nothing but harm to the length of the coat. One problem with all this washing is that it can cause the hair to become dry and brittle, so it pays to dress the whiskers with a little coat conditioner from time to time.

Once the whiskers have grown to a good length, the next problem is to keep them out of the dog's mouth. This can easily be done by drawing them up to each side and tying a little topknot band to hold the resulting bunches out and away from the mouth area. I always think that a Shih Tzu with whiskers dressed in this way looks very oriental, although you must watch that the bands do not cause unsightly kinks in the face furnishings and take care that they are not pulled so tight that they cause discomfort.

To preserve the hair of the topknot, some exhibitors like to use several bands along the length of the hair to hold it to the back of the head, whilst others prefer to plait the hair to achieve the same purpose. Once again, the danger with either of these methods is that they will cause kinks in the coat, so neither should be used immediately before a show.

When you put oils and conditioners on the coat of a show dog, always remember the Kennel Club rule: 'No substance which alters the natural colour, texture or body of the coat may be used in the preparation of a dog for exhibition either before or at the show. Any other substance which may be used in the preparation of a dog for exhibition must not be allowed to remain on a dog at the time of exhibition.' Most of us surely approve of the spirit of this rule and would be greatly opposed to the use of, for example, hair colouring on a mis-marked dog or dye to conceal a lack of pigment. On the other hand, obeying the rule to the letter is difficult if not impossible, for even the mildest of shampoos will undoubtedly alter the texture and body of the coat, as will most of the conditioning preparations that are in common use today. In practice a sort of compromise prevails, with exhibitors using a variety of preparations to keep their dogs' coats clean and free from tangles but at the same time not 'cheating' by seeking to alter the appearance of the coat. Any dog at a show is liable to have a sample of his coat taken for testing for 'forbidden substances' by the Kennel Club, so use common sense and discretion along with your choice of shampoo.

As the whiskers grow, they can be tied clear of the mouth with small 'topknot' bands. (Photo: Yvonne Hyde.)

When the topknot grows to full length, extra bands can be used to keep it clear of the face.

Removing the Coat

One of the most drastic solutions to looking after a Shih Tzu's coat is to remove it completely. Cutting off the long coat is often believed to solve all grooming problems, a misconception, alas, because mats will still appear in the short soft undercoat, and regular grooming is still going to be needed. The coat will also grow again, often amazingly quickly, so once it is cut it will have to be cut again, and again. There are circumstances in which removing the coat does become the best option. The first of these is when caring for all the long hair is becoming so burdensome that it is actually spoiling the relationship between dog and owner. The second is when an elderly Shih Tzu begins to resent the brushing and combing, which does occasionally happen. If such a stage is reached the kindest thing to do is to cut or clip the coat so that the old dog need no longer receive so much grooming attention. Thirdly, if the Shih Tzu's lifestyle or environment is such that the long coat is too much of a liability then the dog will be better off without it; such a situation arose when a friend of mine with two Shih Tzus moved to live on a farm, where she found that the long hair in which she had previously taken such pride became a matted, smelly nightmare no matter how often she

Although his hair has been clipped, this pet dog has been left with enough coat to give him an attractive and unmistakably Shih Tzu appearance. (Photo: David Borrett.)

groomed and bathed. And lastly, the coat may have to be cut off for reasons of health.

Professional dog groomers abound, some working at grooming parlours and others willing to visit the dog at home. Any of these will trim a Shih Tzu with scissors or take off the coat with clippers if preferred. You can buy clippers yourself, but they are rather expensive, and in any case it is possible to produce a perfectly acceptable 'puppy trim' at home using nothing more than a good pair of scissors. Whether the coat is scissored or clipped, do be sure that it is not cut so short as to be virtually shaved, because this breed's hair gives it a degree of protection from both the cold and the sun. I have heard of more than one case of a Shih Tzu with bad sunburn after all its hair had been cut off, indicating that the skin can be quite sensitive if it is overexposed.

Always leave the hair of the head and ears longer, however short the body coat is cut, for this is the way to keep the 'Shih Tzu' look to your dog. Ear furnishings and whiskers look rather nice if they are cut square and level with the chin. The hair round the eyes in particular must never be cut too short, because it may regrow up into the eyes, causing irritation and even infection.

7

Showing

The first ever dog show is believed to have been for Pointers and Setters in 1859. It was held at Newcastle upon Tyne, with sixty dogs entered and three judges for each breed. This small beginning was followed by other shows until, in 1873, the Kennel Club was formed to regulate such events. Dog showing has increased in popularity ever since, with the result that today there is barely a week in the year when at least one show does not take place, and the number of exhibits entered continues to rise year on year. Prize cards are given out, usually to fourth or fifth place in each class, and rosettes are also sometimes on offer. Successful exhibitors cannot expect to grow rich on their winnings, because prize money consists of only a pound or two, or else it is non-existent.

Showing can be a simply marvellous pastime, compelling and pleasurable for the whole family, and can be enjoyed by anyone who is reasonably mobile, from the quite young to the distinctly elderly. Although the cost of entries at shows compares very favourably with that of other hobbies, travelling expenses can be a large drain on the

A group of Shih Tzus at a pre-war show at Olympia.

exhibitor's purse if a lot of shows are attended across a wide area. Another considerable expense can be the equipment that most regular exhibitors find it necessary to acquire: this includes a travelling crate for each dog shown, a box or bag for all the necessary grooming equipment, a folding grooming table, and a sturdy trolley with good-sized wheels for carting all this paraphernalia about at the shows. Sometimes people opt for a combination of the last two, consisting of a table which folds down into a wheeled trolley. A large sunshade is useful in the summer months, together with a 'space blanket' to protect the dogs from the heat. The British climate also makes it advisable to carry waterproof gear to most shows, for the protection of the humans as much as the dogs. The average exhibitor will spend several hundred pounds to buy all the necessary equipment, but dog shows can be attended and indeed enjoyed with very much less expenditure.

Since the same group of people tend to go along to show after show, you soon find that you become familiar with most of them. After a period of attending shows you will pick up literally hundreds of acquaintances and, if you are lucky, a handful of really good friends. I always think of the Shih Tzu showing fraternity as rather like a global village, and it is just as much a mixture of types and personalities as most villages are. It is amazing how people from all walks of life and all countries in the world come together because of their common interest in one particular breed of dog.

Often a newcomer will find that prize cards do not come along very easily – perhaps his or her Shih Tzu is simply not of good enough quality, or the owner has not yet learned how to present and handle him to get the best out of him. But when you first do win a prize your joy will be incomparable, and you may well find yourself hooked on this new way of life. Unfortunately, some exhibitors progress beyond this happy state, becoming greedy for more and more success, and end up valuing their dogs only for the wins they can achieve. As someone who has been to more shows as an observer or organizer than as an exhibitor, I have too often seen people become jealous of the success of others, blind to the faults of their own dogs and bitter when they do not win. The very best advice I can give any newcomer is that when you stop enjoying a day at a show for the experience itself and for the company of like-minded people, then it is the time to find another occupation.

Now that I have referred to some of the negative aspects of dog showing and its adverse effects on some people, you may wonder why I still recommend it as a pastime. One reason is that the undesirable among dog fanciers form only a minority, and it is entirely possible to enjoy yourself to the full by avoiding them. Another is that dog showing has an importance far beyond providing a hobby for dog owners: when we join the showing fraternity we all make a significant contribution to the evolution of the breed we love. From this aspect the value of dog shows to this breed, as to any other, is beyond question; indeed, it is hard to imagine what might become of the Shih Tzu without shows. How would a breeder evaluate his or her progress without going to shows from time to time? Variations in type would proliferate if each breeder was breeding in isolation, whereas when your dog is are standing in line with twenty others of the same breed, variation in type, size and soundness is obvious. This breed has changed greatly over the last fifty years, and doubtless will continue to do so, but at least its development is monitored through the exhibition of Shih Tzus one against another, and by the contact between breeders and enthusiasts that results from this. The breed clubs exist to protect our breed, but here again shows help by providing the impetus for the clubs as well as some of their financial base.

Having acquired a Shih Tzu that they would rather like to show, people often ask 'But where do I start?' They have found the world of dog shows rather confusing and the jargon incomprehensible. My reply is always that this pastime is like any other: you will soon pick it up as you go along. To start with, find out from the Kennel Club where the nearest canine society or Shih Tzu club is located. Then obtain information from the secretary of this local society about its regular events, such as ringcraft classes (where you and your dog can learn how to perform in the show ring), match evenings and shows. Once you have joined up with your local club and gone along to one or two events, you should be able to get plenty of advice on how to set about showing.

Types of Show

All dog shows in the UK are run under licence from the Kennel Club. In order to enter them a dog must be correctly registered with the Kennel Club and must be at least six months old. These rules apply to all the shows described below except exemption shows, which are 'exempt'. Some shows can be entered only by members of a society, which is by no means as exclusive as it may sound, because for a very small annual membership fee it is possible to join any of your local dog show societies, and thereafter you can enter all the shows through the year, attend any of the society's ringcraft sessions and also go to its social events, as well as having the right to vote at the annual general meeting.

There is no need to enter in advance for exemption shows, matches or primary shows. All other shows must be entered in advance on a form provided by the organizers.

Exemption Shows

The exemption show is different from all the other shows held in the UK. Exemption shows are organized in aid of some good cause or other, perhaps a church building fund or as part of a school's fund-raising efforts, and consequently it is not unusual for such shows to be held in conjunction with a fête or bazaar. You just turn up on the day with your dog and choose which classes to enter then and there. The classes will include up to five which are exclusively for pedigree dogs, such as Any Variety Utility or Any Variety Puppy, both of which might be suitable for a Shih Tzu, and these will be followed by a number of classes which are suitable for both pedigree and non-pedigree dogs. The latter are often referred to as the 'fun' classes, such as 'The Dog with the Waggiest Tail', 'The Dog Most Like its Owner' or 'The Dog the Judge would Most Like to Take Home', and dogs do not need to be Kennel Club registered to take part in these. It is in the spirit of these shows to enter lots of classes, as the entry fees are going to a good cause, and usually a good time is had by all, dogs and owners. Most exemption shows are held in the open air, and so good weather is really a prerequisite for those of us who are showing long-haired dogs.

Matches

A match is a form of 'knock-out' competition between members of a dog society or between members of two competing clubs. In order to take part, a dog must be owned by a member of the club or clubs that are running the event. Many of the canine societies run matches regularly for the benefit of their members, not unusually as often as once a month, and these events often take place on a weekday evening. The competition at a match consists of dogs being judged in pairs, one against another, until by a simple process of elimination there are only two left, then finally one becomes 'Best in Match'. Matches provide an ideal opportunity to practise with a dog before going off to one of the bigger and more serious shows, as well as enabling you to meet other local dog fanciers and to get to know something about them and their dogs. Many a friendship has been born at such an event.

Sanction Shows

Entry at a sanction show was limited to members of the society that organized it, and the number of classes could not exceed twenty-five. No class higher than Post Graduate (*see* Show Classes, below) was classified, so dogs that had done a lot of winning could not be exhibited at this sort of show. Years ago these shows were extremely popular, both as pleasant social events and as an ideal opportunity to give a puppy a practice outing, usually on a weekday evening. However, their popularity declined, and owing to this lack of support the Kennel Club discontinued this type of show after 1998.

Primary Shows

Just as at a sanction show, entry at a primary show was confined to members of the society organizing the competition. Entries were taken on the day, and the show was restricted to a maximum of eight classes only, with no dog allowed to take part if he had won a first prize at any show, except for prizes won in puppy classes. This type of show was a comparatively recent innovation on the part of the Kennel Club but it has never been much of a success, which accounts for its abolition.

Limited Shows

This is the third type of show to be confined to members of the organizing society. No dog is allowed to compete if he has won a Challenge Certificate (CC).

Open Shows

As the name suggests, open shows are open to any pedigree dog that is registered with the Kennel Club, including champions, so competition can be extremely tough. None the less, open shows are very popular in the UK, and it is possible to find one within reasonable travelling distance almost every weekend of the year. Classes especially for Shih Tzus will often be scheduled, so your dog will have an opportunity to compete directly against others of the same breed. Depending on the area, the time of the year and the society's choice of judge, an open show may attract a large entry of Shih Tzus or a very small one with only one or two in each class. The latter may make for some easy prize cards, but it really isn't much fun to win without competition. Shih Tzu fanciers should support open shows whenever they can, to keep the breed classes on the schedule. If there are no classes for Shih Tzus, you can still enter an open show in 'Not Separately Classified', which is the class for breeds that have no classes of their own. There will also be some variety classes in which all breeds compete together. Sometimes an open show is run in conjunction with an agricultural show, which makes a good day out for the whole family.

Championship Shows

Last we come to the really big shows, the only ones where a dog may win a Challenge Certificate (CC). A dog that has won three CCs under separate judges earns the title of Champion. All the breed clubs

Winners from the dog classes line up for the challenge, City of Birmingham 1993. The CC winner (left-hand side) was Crowvalley The Chancer, owned and bred by Les and Betty Williams. (Photo: Audrey Dadds.)

run one championship show each year exclusively for the Shih Tzu, whilst general championship shows schedule classes for many other breeds. The latter shows usually last more than one day. At each championship show there will be only two CCs for Shih Tzus, one for the best dog and one for the best bitch. The judge can also award Reserve Challenge Certificates to the second-best dog and bitch, and in the event that either of the CC winners is disqualified then the Reserve CC winner receives the CC instead.

After the two CCs have been awarded, the judge of the day selects the better of the two winners to be Best of Breed, and this dog then goes on to compete against other breeds in the Utility Group. The Utility Group contains the three sizes of Poodle, Dalmatians, Bulldogs, Chow Chows and Lhasa Apsos as well as Shih Tzus and other breeds, so it is a mixed bag and consequently difficult to win. To compete for the Best in Show award the Shih Tzu must first win this Group.

It is common for more than a hundred Shih Tzus to attend any one championship show, and sometimes twice that number will be at a breed club show, so it can be seen that a first prize does not come easily. For the serious exhibitor, these are the shows that really count, and real enthusiasts travel the length and breadth of the land to enter as many as possible each year. They are also the most expensive to enter. Crufts is probably the best known of the general championship shows in the UK. General championship shows are normally benched, which is to say that each dog is allocated a raised platform on which he should be fastened for the duration of the show while he is not in the ring. The bench is usually about 2ft (60cm) wide, so most of the travelling crates used for Shih Tzus will fit onto this, and can be used to keep the dog confined in safety.

Entering a Show

Forthcoming shows are advertised in the weekly dog papers *Dog World* and *Our Dogs*. You can buy them from newsagents, but will probably need to order them in advance. Show advertisements give details of the date and venue, and of the judge or judges who will be officiating, together with the closing date before which entries must be received, and the telephone number of the show secretary. Ring the secretary to get hold of a show schedule, which is a booklet containing details of the show and an entry form. Complete the entry form with details of your dog and its breeding, and post it off in good time. In the case of the championship shows the closing date for entries can be many weeks in advance of the show, so this needs to be noted. This does not apply to exemption shows and others which can be entered on the day, and for which no forward planning is needed.

Show Classes

The most common mistake made by the new exhibitor is to enter too many classes, especially with a puppy. Except at an exemption show, which is run for fun and is a different matter altogether, it is usually sufficient to enter one or two classes at most. Where separate classes are scheduled for dogs and for bitches, the dog classes are always judged first. The following classes may be scheduled at open and championship shows, and it can be seen that there is a natural progression whereby an exhibit will move from class to class as he grows older and wins more and more.

Minor Puppy

This class may be entered only by puppies of six calendar months of age and not exceeding nine calendar months of age on the first day of the show.

Puppy

For puppies of six and not exceeding twelve months on the first day of the show.

Junior

For dogs of six and not exceeding eighteen calendar months of age on the first day of the show.

Novice

For dogs that have not won a CC or three or more first prizes at open and championship shows, except for prizes won in the puppy classes. Note that there is no age restriction with this class, but that a dog's eligibility is determined by what he has won.

Post Graduate

For dogs that have not won a Challenge Certificate or five or more first prizes at championship shows in Post Graduate, Minor Limit, Mid-Limit, Limit or Open classes, whether restricted or not.

Limit

For dogs that have not won three Challenge Certificates under three different judges or seven or more first prizes in all at championship shows in Limit or Open classes confined to the breed, whether restricted or not, at shows where Challenge Certificates were offered for the breed.

Open

For all dogs of the breed for which the class is provided and eligible for entry at the show.

Choosing the Right Class

Many other classes may be scheduled at a show, but the above examples taken from the classification for a championship show are the most common, and show how the Kennel Club has carefully defined the classes so that the competition in each class is stiffer than in the preceding one. It should be obvious from this that it is rather foolhardy to enter your dog in a class such as Limit when the number of prizes he has won make him eligible for Novice, yet one sees inexperienced or overambitious exhibitors doing just this at many of the shows. This is not to say that there is never a good reason for entering in a class other than the lowest for which one's Shih Tzu is eligible, just that it is not a wise course for the beginner. For example, a more experienced exhibitor will perhaps choose to enter a Junior dog in the Post Graduate class, but he may be doing this in the knowledge that his exhibit is rather oversized for his age and will therefore look less out of place in a class with the older dogs. Sometimes a wily exhibitor will enter his Novice dog in Open in the hope of fooling the judge into believing that his dog has enjoyed more success than is actually the case, but he plays this game at his peril, and few judges will be duped!

Ringcraft

I have already mentioned ringcraft classes in Chapter 4, recommending them for show and non-show puppies alike as a way of socializing the dog with others of various breeds. For the puppy that is intended for the show ring, such classes are a vital part of the preparation. Exhibitors in other European countries have told me that they greatly envy UK exhibitors for their regular (often weekly) ringcraft classes, which are inexpensive and enjoyable to attend, and which are usually very well run.

The lessons that the potential show puppy must learn include how to stand still and calmly on the table to be examined by a judge. This examination involves handling from head to tail and an inspection of the teeth. Apart from practising this in a formal ringcraft situation, I find it helpful to get a puppy used to such handling by examining him on an almost daily basis, and since the puppy must permit anyone – not just his owner – to inspect him, I often ask visitors to spare a minute or two to 'play the judge' for the benefit of my latest pup. As well as standing on the table the show dog is required to stand in line with the other dogs in the ring and adopt what is known as the 'show pose' in which he stands four-square with his head and tail held high to present the best possible picture of himself. This means that the dog must also learn to ignore other dogs when necessary. Many of the photographs in this book show Shih Tzus in the show pose.

Puppy and handler must perfect their team skills in order that they work together when the exhibit is required to move. When all the exhibitors are asked to move together in a big circle round the outside of the ring, you and your dog must match your pace to that of the dog in front, and you therefore have to be able to move smartly at various speeds. On the other hand, when you are asked to move your dog individually, you have an opportunity to choose your pace to suit yourselves, and the whole performance will look much better if lots of practice has been put into achieving the right effect.

It is a mistake to try to train and school a young puppy to perfection too quickly. The normal puppy is unlikely to show straight away, usually feeling inclined to leap about and to play or investigate everything that is going on rather than standing still. The important thing is that a puppy should find showing to be fun. The owner who tries to do too much too soon runs the danger of making the puppy bored or unhappy, or both. Then the tail goes down and you no longer have a show puppy.

At the Show

Assuming that a dog has been taught what will be required of it and that the coat has been properly prepared, the new exhibitor will be ready to take those first exciting steps into the show ring. The first show can be nerve-racking, but you can do a lot to make the day go smoothly.

Before taking a Shih Tzu to its first show, try to attend at least one similar type of show just to watch what goes on. This will help you to become familiar with the way such a show is organized so that you won't feel so lost when you actually go as an exhibitor. On the night before the big event, prepare everything you need, making a check-list of all that needs to be taken. Some people pack their car before they go to bed so that in the morning they have only themselves and the dogs to remember.

Always make an early start, to allow for traffic delays: there is nothing worse than arriving at a show late and finding you have missed your class. On arrival at the show, enquire where and when the Shih Tzus are to be judged, and locate the ring at once, before finding your bench if it is a benched show, or a spot to set up your grooming table if there is no benching. Ideally the grooming table should be in sight of the ring, but above all it must not impede any gangway – you will soon become unpopular if you start off by getting in everybody's way. Each exhibitor has to wear a ring number – a card bearing their dog's competition number. You need to find

A class of exhibitors in the ring at the City of Birmingham Championship Show, 1993. (Photo: Audrey Dadds.)

out whether you will be given your number by the steward in the ring, or whether it is on the bench.

Always attend to the needs of your dog first. He may need exercising to relieve himself, especially if you have travelled a long way, and perhaps he would like a drink of water. You will have prepared your Shih Tzu's long coat thoroughly the evening before, grooming right through and bathing if necessary, but have another grooming session as the time for your class draws near. Some exhibitors take an impressive number of grooming aids such as portable hair-dryers to shows, but this is really not necessary so long as you have done your preparation well at home. Leave retying the topknot until last, but allow time to do it more than once as nervousness may make your first attempt a bit lopsided.

Keep an eye on the progress in the ring, so that you are ready to go in as soon as your first class is called. It is very bad manners to keep the judge waiting, and he may not necessarily wait for you in any case. Once dogs and exhibitors are in the ring, with their ring numbers in place, everyone stands their dogs whilst the judge walks round and takes a first careful look at the assembled exhibits. The judge may or may not ask all the exhibitors to move their dogs round the ring in a big circle; if you have been keeping an eye on the previous classes you will have noted the normal procedure and will be ready for it.

In the Ring

Next, each dog is placed on the table to be examined, and then the exhibitor is asked to walk him, either up and down or in a triangle according to the judge's instructions. Many new exhibitors have told me that they feel particularly self-conscious when it comes to walking their dog alone in the centre of the ring, but I always assure them that if people are watching they will have their eyes on the dog and not them, just as the judge does. Once this is accepted, the beginner will feel much less conspicuous and will be better able to concentrate on the job in hand.

In a large class, let your dog relax while the others are having their turn, but be on the alert for the approach of the end of the class, when your dog must once again be standing and looking his very best as the judge comes along to select the winners. It is perfectly all right to take a brush or a comb into the ring so that you can get the dog's coat looking immaculate again for this final moment, but avoid getting into the habit of brushing away incessantly: it is very distracting for a judge and may prove counterproductive. Sometimes at this final stage a judge will ask some of the exhibits to move once more, so be ready for this to happen and respond smartly to the judge's instructions.

At the end of your first class you may find yourself 'in the cards', in which case your exuberance will know no bounds. Taking a prize card home from your first show is pretty special, so enjoy the experience to the full. There is nothing quite like it, I assure you. But what if you don't win? Perhaps you nearly did, but didn't put in just as good a performance as the winners did, or maybe your dog was not as good as the others in the opinion of the judge of the day. Judges vary greatly in their assessment of individual exhibits, so things may be very different next time out. Remember that no one wins all the time, not even the most famous and successful of exhibitors. Above all, remember that you are taking home exactly the same dog that you set out with in the morning, and that prizes, or the lack of them, do not alter a dog in any way at all. If you have faith in the quality of your dog, then pity the judge who could not see his virtues and look forward to the next show.

Sometimes exhibitors like to ask a judge's opinion of an unplaced dog after judging is completed. If you do this, be prepared to accept the judge's comments with a good grace, once again remembering that this is only one person's opinion.

Tricks of the Trade

The skilful handler is one who presents a dog to the best possible advantage, enhancing the good points and making this look quite easy. A simple example of clever handling is choosing where to stand among the other exhibits when going into a class. If your dog is on the small size, standing him between two large ones will only serve to accentuate this, so try to place yourself between two exhibits of the smaller type.

An exhibitor who is aware that his or her Shih Tzu is rather longer in the back than makes for ideal balance may try to compensate for this in the line-up. Instead of standing the dog square on to the centre of the ring, he may choose to stand the forequarters a little forward of the rear, thus presenting the judge with a slightly foreshortened picture of the exhibit. One or two exhibitors try, when standing their dogs in the ring, to lift a flat tail by slipping their fingers under it, but this seems a little pointless, because the flat tail carriage is going to be evident anyway once the dog is on the move.

In some breeds it is common to take a variety of titbits into the ring, with which to tempt the dog and keep him on his toes, but I have never seen this done much in the Shih Tzu ring. If it works for you and your dog then try it by all means, but on no account let your own use of titbits distract the other exhibits in the ring.

Be observant at all times when in the ring. At one show I noticed a Shih Tzu that walked considerably better than any of the others in the class, for the simple reason that the handler had spotted a nasty rut in the grass and carefully led his dog around it. The other six exhibitors had taken their dogs straight across the dip, so that by the time they had settled back into a steady gait each dog's chance to show off his soundness of movement was lost. The observant and thoughtful exhibitor won his class, not only because he had a good dog but also because he had shown him to the best possible advantage.

The good exhibitor should always be considerate of his dog. At some of the outdoor summer shows the heat can quickly build up so that it becomes uncomfortable for such a heavily coated breed as the Shih Tzu. In these circumstances, you have to hope that judges will exercise their right to carry out their duties under cover, but if they don't then it is your right to withdraw from the class rather than stand there and watch your dog endure distress from the heat. Sadly, I have yet to see all of the exhibitors putting the welfare of their dogs first in this way in these circumstances, although many of them do at least make sure that they stand so that their own shadows are cast over the dog's back, in an attempt to give some relief.

Each dog must be moved at his own pace to show him off to the best advantage. Many exhibitors let themselves be pressured into emulating the pace set by a previous exhibitor, doing themselves no favours in the process. Once the ideal pace has been found, stick to this regardless of what others may be doing.

Something that should not be forgotten is your own appearance, which should complement that of the dog. Always dress neatly, with suitable shoes and appropriate clothing, and remember that a black dog will virtually disappear against a pair of black trousers. In this instance colour contrast is more effective than colour co-ordination. Pockets are extremely convenient for carrying the brush, titbits or whatever else you feel you need to take into the ring.

One of the best ways to pick up the techniques of showing is to watch classes in which you are not entered yourself. See how the

Ch. Kuire Secret Simon, owned and bred by Josephine Johnson, was the author's choice for Best of Breed in 1985 at the Scottish Kennel Club Show. Josephine dreaded getting Best of Breed with Simon because, although he showed so well in the ring with other Shih Tzus, he detested being in the group ring with other breeds!

Ch. Kareth Kismet of Lyre, bred by Francis Hickey in Ireland and owned by Jim Peat in Scotland, won most of her 15 CCs in England. Shih Tzu breeders pay little regard to distance and national borders!

successful exhibitors manage things, and watch for the less adept. When you see someone making an obvious mistake, stop and ask yourself if you have been doing this. You may also be able to ask someone to video one of your classes: studying such a piece of video is likely to be very educational, even though it may also be a bit depressing at first!

Titles

Champion

Before a dog may be called a Champion he must have won three CCs under three separate judges, and one of the three CCs must have been won when the dog was over the age of twelve months. CCs may be won only at shows with championship status. The CC is often referred to as 'the ticket', a piece of show jargon that can sometimes be rather confusing to the beginner. (A well-known exhibitor in Shih Tzus once took home three tickets: one was the Bitch CC, the second was the Dog CC, and the third was a speeding ticket collected from the police on the M1 on the way to the show. This sort of enthusiasm should definitely be avoided.)

Gaining a title with a Shih Tzu is never easy, and may be harder in the UK than in any other country, but the difficulty varies from year to year according to the stiffness of the competition. On average, about eight or ten new champions are made up in one year. Once a dog gains the title of Champion he is able to continue to compete for further CCs so long as the owner wishes, so the ticket winner at any one show may have had to beat several Champions in order to take the award. In many other countries, such as Sweden or Germany, it is common to have a separate class for Champions, which makes it considerably easier to win a CC.

Junior Warrant

The title of JW (Junior Warrant) may be added to a young dog's name when he has gained a total of twenty-five points between the ages of six and eighteen months. At least twelve of these points must be won at championship shows where CCs are on offer for the breed, and at least twelve gained at championship shows without CCs, or at open shows. Three points are awarded for each first prize at a championship show

Moondreams at Mirazian (left) just after she won her JW at eight months. On the right is Ch. & Ir. Ch. Mirazian Sweet Innocence, who gained her title at the age of seven years. Both are owned by Marjorie Devine.

Ch. Jardhu Myz-Sunn won his JW, then went on to gain his title in 1991. Owned and bred by Jim and Vicki Grugan. (Photo: David Lindsey.)

where CCs are on offer, but only one point is awarded for each first prize at an open show, and no JW points at all may be claimed in respect of a class which has less than three exhibits present.

JW points may be claimed only from one show on any one day, with three clear days between qualifying shows. This rule was devised to prevent puppies being taken to show after show in an attempt to qualify for the JW. Before the rule was introduced, this deplorable practice was not uncommon. Indeed, some foolish people even boasted of having won a 'double' JW, by which they meant that they had amassed fifty or more points. There was no such thing as a double JW, but this sort of nonsense inevitably resulted in some puppies being grossly overshown.

Breed Record Holder

One Shih Tzu has won more Kennel Club Challenge Certificates than any other. Ch. Jardhu The Republican (sired by Bellakerne Dandi of Jardhu out of Huxlor Personality Plus of Jardhu), was bred by Jim and Vicki Grugan and lives with them in Ayrshire. Born in 1992,

Jardhu The Republican, the puppy aged nine months (Photo: Alan Walker.)

Ch. Jardhu The Republican, aged two years, bred and owned by Jim and Vicki Grugan, went on to become the holder of the Breed Record. (Photo: Alan Walker.)

'Repp', as he is known to his friends, has won thirty-seven CCs, each of them under a different judge. Along with all his CCs, Repp has won many other awards, including many Best in Shows, and he has travelled with Jim and Vicki all over the UK to do so. From his puppyhood he showed promise of what was to come, winning the award for Top Shih Tzu puppy in 1993, and he went on to be the top sire in the breed for 1994. Repp has two champion brothers, one in Ireland and one in Sweden. He is a classically marked gold and white.

The Stud Book

Some of the prizes referred to in this chapter entitle a dog to receive a stud book number, a distinction that qualifies the dog for entry to Crufts for life, and also for an entry in the stud book. Dogs without a stud book number must qualify anew each year to enter Crufts. The stud book is a handsome red-bound volume which is published annually by the Kennel Club and which provides an invaluable source for the serious student of any breed. Details of each dog's pedigree are included, as well as a list of his qualifying wins for the year. As I write, for a Shih Tzu to qualify for entry in the stud book he must have won a CC, a Reserve CC or a Junior Warrant, or he must have taken first, second or third in the Open or Limit class at a championship show where CCs were on offer for the breed. Occasionally over the years the qualifications for stud book entry have been varied.

Crufts

If there is one show which is better known than any other and where exhibitors most covet the prizes on offer, this must surely be the Kennel Club's own show, Crufts. Crufts was first staged under the auspices of the Kennel Club in 1948, but had previously been run by Charles Cruft, the talented entrepreneur from whom it takes its name. This is a show at which every dog entered must either have a stud book number or have won certain specified awards at a championship show during the preceding year even to get through the door, a requirement that was introduced in the mid-1960s to restrict the numbers of dogs.

The Shih Tzu was first scheduled with classes at Crufts in 1936, and in those early years most of the top winners belonged to Lady Brownrigg of the Taishan kennel. After the war, Gay Widdrington was extremely successful at Crufts, winning both dog and bitch CC in 1951 and repeating this achievement in 1955. Antarctica dogs won both CCs in 1965 and 1968, as did the Greenmoss kennel in 1972. The first Crufts group winner in the breed was Ch. Harropine Charka Khan at Antarctica.

Les Williams and his late wife Stephanie made up their most famous champion, Ch. Crowvalley Tweedledum, in 1976. Tweedledum, who was also the first champion from Wales, went on to win Reserve in the Utility Group at Crufts on two occasions, and was a great favourite with me, a magnificent gold/white dog with terrific ring presence. After Stephanie's untimely death, Les Williams married Betty Taylor, herself a Shih Tzu exhibitor with the kennel name of Boufalls, and together they have continued the success of the Crowvalley name into the 1990s.

Susan and David Crossley (Santosha kennel) won both CCs in 1988 with Ch. Firefox of Santosha and Ch. Santosha Tiger Lily. Ch. Firefox

Ch. Crowvalley Tweedledum, Reserve Group winner at Crufts in 1977 and again in 1980. Owned and bred by Les and Stephanie Williams. (Photo: L. Young.)

of Santosha, bred by Messrs Easdon and Martin, was the holder of the breed record from 1988 to 1994 with thirty-five CCs, including another at Crufts in 1991. He was the sire of eight champions. Sadly, he died at the comparatively early age of ten, or he might well have sired more. I had a particular affection for Firefox – his son and grandson, together with his great grand-daughter in recent months, have been at my side throughout the writing of this book. The grand-sire of Firefox, Ch. Santosha Sunking, was also a good producer, with seven champion children to his credit, and Sunking in his turn had been a Crufts top winner in 1984 (*see* colour section).

In 1979, Sheila and Tom Richardson won both CCs with Ch. Bellakerne Zipperty Do and Ch. Bellakerne Inca Do, and they also won the CC in 1993 with Ch. Bellakerne Misty Do. On the latter occasion the judge was Jim Peat, who had himself won a CC at Crufts eleven years earlier with Ch. Kareth Khoir Angel.

In 1997 I judged at Crufts myself, a special occasion with many happy memories. With a beautiful entry, including more than twenty champions, I was spoiled for choice, but in the end I chose Ch. Emrose Michelin Man for Best Dog and Best of Breed, and Ch. Hashanah The Immaculate for the Best Bitch. Photographs of both are shown in the colour section. A list of the main winners at Crufts from 1968 to 1998 is shown in Appendix II.

*Ch. Santosha Sunking, Best
of Breed at Crufts in 1984,
was owned and bred by Sue
and David Crossley.*

*Ch. Jardhu Waffles Wu,
winner of the Challenge
Certificate at Crufts in 1985,
bred and owned by Jim and
Vicki Grugan (Photo:
David J. Lindsey.)*

Some of the Shih Tzus that have won top awards at Crufts have gone on to become champions afterwards, but some (a minority) never did. And a few of the most successful Shih Tzus in the breed just never did take a top award at Crufts, which makes the show all the more fascinating.

Children and Dog Shows

I began this chapter by describing dog showing as an activity for the whole family, and end it by referring to the extent to which children can take part. Not only can any child handle a dog in the ring and compete against all the adult exhibitors, but at many of the shows there are also special classes aimed specifically at the junior handler. In these classes it is the youngster's ability to show the dog which is judged, not the dog itself.

Ch. Bellakerne Zippity Do, and Ch. Bellakerne Inca Do, brother and sister Challenge Certificate winners at Crufts in 1979, owned and bred by Sheila and Tom Richardson.

Ch. Kareth Khoir Angel, bred and owned by Jim Peat, was the first solid-gold champion in the breed.

Membership of the Kennel Club Junior Organization is open to all children between the ages of eight and eighteen, and is not expensive. It runs activities on a regional basis, and with its declared aims of promoting 'courtesy, sportsmanship, loyalty and self-discipline' it helps to prepare young people for more than just responsible dog ownership. We have had many splendid young people on the British show scene over the years. Some have gone on to become exhibitors and judges as adults, and all have shown the grown-ups a thing or two when it came to professionalism in the show ring, as well as good manners outside it.

126

8

Judging

It is a truth universally acknowledged that a dog exhibitor in posses-
sion of a year or two's experience in the show ring must be in want of
a judging appointment. This, with apologies to the inestimable Jane
Austen, is how it sometimes appears, so great is the compulsion
that seems to be felt by so many of our exhibitors to embark on a
judging career. To be invited to pass an opinion on other people's
dogs is at once a great privilege and a heavy responsibility. The
future of the breed lies to a large extent in the hands of its judges and
on their ability to assess quality in exhibits and measure them accurately against the Breed Standard, yet the vast majority of new judges
leap into the ring long before they are ready to take on this task. For a
long time there were no specific qualifications for dog judges in
Britain, something that was only seriously addressed by the Kennel
Club as recently as 1997. That said, even in those countries where
judges have had to undergo detailed training and examinations, there
is no certainty that only competent judges officiate.

What qualifies someone to judge dogs, if it is not a simple matter of
passing examinations? Certainly knowledge, both theoretical and
practical, is an essential qualification. Practical knowledge is in part
gained through owning, showing and breeding good Shih Tzus.
Although some of the cleverest breeders and exhibitors have not
always made the best judges, none the less non-specialist judges – that
is to say those who have never owned the breed – tend to fall short,
particularly when it comes to assessing puppies and sometimes when
judging the dog rather than the hairdressing. Much has been written
over the years about the need for judges to have 'an eye for a good
dog', an elusive ability that cannot be taught. However, if the innate
ability to spot quality is there, it will always increase with experience.

Knowledge is of little use without the ability to apply it in the
judging situation, and this depends on a combination of skills. Judges
need the ability to make cool and detached assessments, as well as an
excellent memory and a systematic approach. Mental stamina is

required to concentrate on class after class without any lapses, perhaps all day at a championship show. The courage to make decisions without fear or favour is also required, especially when this can cost old friendships. Judges should have integrity, a quality that cannot be given or learnt, though I happen to believe that it can be strengthened in a variety of ways. From the time when you start going to shows, learn to turn away from those who criticize all dogs other than their own, and from those whose happiness lies in character assassination of the judge of the day, and you will be getting your 'integrity muscles' into good shape.

Judging also requires physical stamina, because it can be very tiring standing all day in the ring, moving up and down to view the dogs from different angles and bending down to floor level at frequent intervals to take a second, close look. Most of us with a lot of judging experience can tell tales of judging in the teeming rain or in sweltering sunshine, in dark corners of tents or on ground so uneven that we could hardly see the movement of the dogs. This is not a job for the faint-hearted or the delicate.

Judges' Training

There are lots of ways in which would-be judges can train themselves for the job. These include reading extensively on the subject, attending seminars, stewarding, observation and practice. Such preparation will be time well spent.

In addition to reading books about the Shih Tzu, it can be enlightening to read about other breeds and about the conformation and anatomy of the canine species generally. Suggestions for further reading are given at the end of this book, but this is a starting point only. Most of the breed clubs publish magazines two or three times a year, and they often have high topical and educational articles by experts, pointing out the latest trends in the breed and discussing current concerns. Rather than merely reading the Breed Standard over and over again, try writing notes to elaborate on the various points, much as I have done in Chapter 2. No two people are likely to write exactly the same comments, but the exercise does help to clarify one's thoughts. Write another set of notes a year later, and you will probably find that your increased experience has caused your emphasis to change.

Most of the Shih Tzu breed clubs have in recent years organized seminars, or 'teach-ins' as they are sometimes called, for judges and would-be judges. The most common format is to have half the day devoted to lectures given by breed specialists, and the remainder of the time given over to 'hands-on' experience. This enables those attending to 'go over' Shih Tzus (which means examining them as judges do) in order to try to put the theory into practice. Valuable though these events are, they sometimes produce novice judges with a tendency to 'fault judge' – that is, being able to recognize such faults as a poor mouth or a flat tail but not so good at spotting quality. Judges who pick the dogs with the fewest faults may end up with mediocre specimens for their prizewinners. Good seminars teach a more positive approach, together with skills such as how to make a systematic assessment and how to compare one dog against another.

Stewarding

Stewarding is the best way to learn many of the skills involved in judging, besides being a helpful contribution to the dog game. I am pleased that the Kennel Club looks set to insist on stewarding experience as a prerequisite to a judging career. A steward's job is to assist the judge. He will prepare all the paperwork, and check that all the exhibitors are present and that their dogs have been properly entered into the class. He is also responsible for the general smooth running of the process, without interfering with the actual judging.

The first benefit to be gained from stewarding is that it helps to dissipate any self-consciousness that might arise from standing there in the middle of the ring. A steward is much too busy to be embarrassed about taking up such a conspicuous position, and it very soon becomes second nature to get on with the job in hand, oblivious to the ringsiders. Secondly, you learn a lot about ring management and show procedure, so that when that first judging appointment comes along you will be able to take control of the ring without even having to think about it. Thirdly, a judge with stewarding experience is equipped to cope with the unfortunate, but by no means unknown, situation in which he finds that he has been landed with an inadequate steward and has to do both jobs.

A ring steward is also in a very good situation to learn by observation. Even stewarding for a bad judge can be extremely educational, so long as you are aware of the situation. For the aspiring judge of the Shih Tzu, it can be beneficial to steward for other breeds, such as the Whippet or perhaps the Chinese Crested: if you have studied your anatomy and conformation, watching breeds such as these at close quarters is really informative because you can see the interaction of muscle and bone in action very much better than you ever will watching a long-coated breed. It is also informative to get a close look at breeds such as the Pekingese, Lhasa Apso and Tibetan Spaniel, which share some characteristics with the Shih Tzu.

An efficient, methodical steward, with the unobtrusive knack of being everywhere at once, is a great asset to any judge, and stewards who reach that level of proficiency are always in demand. For the steward it is a real pleasure to work with a good judge. From the judge's point of view, a good steward is invaluable, especially when working under pressure to get through a large entry. On the other hand, an officious steward may be more of a liability than an asset: more than once ringside criticism has arisen when steward and judge have found it necessary to consult together before the judge made any decisions, most recently in 1997 when on one occasion exhibitors seemed unsure about which of the two officials was actually making the decisions. The two activities, stewarding and judging, are not mutually exclusive at any level, but they are separate activities and should be seen to be so.

Observation and Practice

Years ago, the rules of showing prevented any exhibitors from leaving a show until towards the end of the day. We all stayed to watch classes other than our own, and even other breeds, and above all we talked together and looked at each others' dogs. It is only now, when people are permitted to leave as soon as their dog has been into the ring, and often do so, that I realize just how valuable those afternoons were when it came to the accumulation of knowledge.

A good mental exercise for aspiring judges is to watch and mentally 'judge' at least one whole class at every show they attend. Try to sit in line with the spot from which the judge is working, to obtain a good view of exhibits on the move. You will not be able to examine the dogs on the table, but an attempt to place four or five as the winners is still a useful exercise, and will build up your powers of concentration. The imaginary placings made in this way will be based on soundness and style in movement, on balance, on the carriage of head and tail and on the ratio of length to height. More can be seen from the ringside than at first seems possible, as you learn to take in more and more.

Take the opportunity to go over dogs at home with your own Shih Tzus, examining them on a table as if you are judging. Do this on a daily basis until you have built up a pattern which comes naturally, so that you start each time in the same place, covering the same points in the same order. Going over a dog does not necessitate conducting some sort of pseudo-veterinary examination by prodding and poking every inch of the unfortunate animal, a practice that is a sure sign of an inexperienced judge. On the other hand, it does require more than a cursory pat or two, which suggests either lack of interest or confusion about where to begin.

Because of the heavy coat, judging a Shih Tzu involves more handling than with some other breeds. On the head, because the arrangement of a topknot can create a deceptive appearance, you have to feel for the skull shape with the fingertips, and the same applies to the depth of the stop. To look at the teeth and the bite, just lift the top lip gently from above with forefinger and thumb on each side of the mouth. The lay of the shoulders can be found with a touch of the hand. You will need to check the shape of the whole front assembly carefully. An easy way to do this is to run both hands down the front legs to check the bone and the degree of straightness that can be found there. This breed should have a good spring of rib, but sometimes a dog will appear to have good width when in fact its coat is rather matted, so check for this with the fingers. It is sufficient merely to flick the tail aside to see if the topline is level as the dog stands. At the rear of a dog, feel for muscle tone and angulation, and lastly check a male for the presence of two fully descended testicles.

Sometimes it is difficult for a novice judge to estimate a dog's height at the withers by sight, but there is a trick to this. Place your arm in a vertical position perpendicular to a table, with the middle finger pressed firmly to the table top, and measure 10½in (26.7cm) up your arm from the table. Now work out a way of remembering exactly where this point comes on your arm. This method can be useful as a rough guide in judging until the novice gains more experience and confidence, but should only be used when really necessary. Suppose, for example, that you are trying to decide between two dogs of equal merit, one of which looks as if it may be well over the size required by the Standard. Just reaching over the withers to touch the floor by the dog will help to confirm your suspicion that this dog is indeed considerably taller than it should be, and this may be the deciding factor in a close decision.

It is a matter of regret to me that student judges are not allowed into the ring in Britain. The reason given has always been that it is not possible with our large entries, yet it is allowed in certain countries where entries have become comparable to ours in recent years. I wonder whether the ill-fated primary show, which has never really taken off as a viable proposition, could not have been allocated to the breed clubs specifically as an event at which student judges could be introduced.

On the occasions when I have agreed to have a student judge in my ring (both in Sweden and in Germany), it seemed to me to be an exceptionally worthwhile exercise, one that was good for me too as it sharpened my perceptions to have to explain my reasoning as I went along. As judge I examined each dog on the table before the student did, and then we both watched him move before writing an individual critique. At the end of the class, the student wrote down his placings before I made my awards, and then we discussed the results briefly before the next class began. Finally, I had to write an assessment on the student judge's knowledge and performance. It made for a long day for everyone, including the dogs and their owners, but some of the latter told me that they accepted this in such a good natured way because they knew it was to their own advantage in the long run.

Selection of Judges

In future, when a British club or society schedules more than three classes for Shih Tzus, the judge appointed will have to be chosen from those who are named in the breed club lists of approved judges. All breed clubs maintain judging lists of the names of people they consider to be suitable to judge at the various levels, perhaps with one list of those approved to judge at open shows and another of those approved to judge at championship show level. Inclusion in these lists has not always been based solely on merit, and some committees have on occasion let politics or personalities creep into their deliberations. The Kennel Club is policing the procedures more rigidly, however. Just as important is that anyone who does accept a judging invitation for the first time should be absolutely sure that he or she is ready for this step. In the past, when anyone could accept an invititation to judge, without reference to any qualifications, it was not uncommon for people to leap into the centre of the ring long before they were ready to do so. Remember that judges are put under scrutiny themselves, often by people who themselves have many years of experience in the breed.

The Mechanics of Judging

This is one area where any judge can get it right. Some of the things I shall mention may seem glaringly obvious, yet in all of them some judges to my certain knowledge have failed to meet even the minimum standard. The process begins with the invitation to judge, which should be answered promptly and filed with a copy of your reply. This first exchange of letters constitutes a contract between the judge and the society that is running the show. A further letter will be sent to you nearer to the date of the show, giving details of the entry and times of judging, and often a map of how to reach the venue.

By the day before the show, you should know exactly what route to take to reach the venue and have made a decision on the vexed question of what to wear. Lots of judges come unstuck here, either dressing as if for a day of gardening, or going to the other extreme of arriving as if about to take part in a fashion show. Choose between these two extremes, dressing for simplicity, smartness and comfort. Avoid flapping skirts and sleeves, clanking jewellery and huge hats, all of which may well alarm the dogs and distract them from their showing. I once saw a lady attempting to judge with one hand clamped to her indisputably lovely hat to prevent it from flying off in a stiff breeze, while three-quarters of the dogs being exhibited were shying away in alarm whenever she came near them.

Arrive at the show really early, having allowed more than enough time for the journey in case of traffic hold-ups. Report at once to the secretary, because show secretaries need to know that their judges have arrived safely. You will probably get a cup of coffee, and will be given your judging book at this stage. The ring numbers of all the dogs entered are printed in the judging book, class by class, and beside each list of numbers there are three columns for the results. One column stays in the book for the judge to refer to, one will end up in the secretary's hands and the third will be torn out and displayed at the ringside as soon as each class is completed. The second two slips, which are detachable, must be signed by the judge before they are removed from the book at the end of each class.

Find the judging ring well before the classes are scheduled to begin, and introduce yourself to the stewards if you have not already met them. If there is another judge in the ring ahead of you do not on any account enter the ring until judge and stewards have finished their work. Once the ring is free, walk round it to check for any hazards such as broken glass, which you should pick up, or hollows in which dogs or exhibitors might stumble. In the case of the latter you should plan to send the dogs round on a route that avoids the bad ground. The table on which the dogs are to be examined should also be checked to make sure that it does not rock or wobble, as the dogs will feel very insecure unless the table is secure. On one occasion I arrived in my ring to find that the table was so rickety that it nearly fell over when I put my bag on it, so I persuaded one of the exhibitors to lend her sturdy grooming table and we used that all day. The last thing to do before starting to judge is to make sure the stewards know exactly how you wish the ring to be organized, where dogs coming through from a previous class should stand, and so on. Be sure that you are aware how many prizes are to be awarded in each class, as there is nothing worse than calling out five winners only to discover that there are just four prize cards.

Any absentees in a class must be noted as such on the slips in the judging book. Although a steward will often offer to do this it is the responsibility of the judge alone. For each class to be judged, follow the same pattern so that your exhibitors can see what is required of them. Thus, if you want to walk all the exhibits round in a circle before examining them individually, do this in every class and not just in some. Remember also to keep to a consistent pattern when examining the dogs on the table, so that you can be seen to give them all the same attention. When going over the dogs on the table, never just pounce on them unannounced but approach calmly from the front. Many judges offer the back of their hand for the dog to smell before actually putting their hands on him. If you have occasion to speak to exhibitors, do so politely and with courtesy, remembering that they have paid you a compliment by bringing these dogs for you to judge, and that without them there would be no show.

After examining each dog on the table, ask the exhibitor to move him. To have the dogs moved in a triangle is ideal because this enables you to see the rear action as the dog sets off, then the profile view as it is taken across the second leg of the triangle, and finally the front movement as the exhibitor comes back towards you. Depending on the size and shape of the ring, this is not always feasible, so be prepared to be flexible, and if there is only room for the dogs to move straight up and down, ask for it to be done twice, and move to the side to get the profile view. Viewing a dog's movement from the side is essential for a proper assessment of its front extension, topline, head carriage and balance.

A good judge must always be aware of what is going on around the ring and prepared to take this into account. For example, if someone

Tom Richardson judges Sheila Rabson's dog at WELKS
Championship Show, 1998.

drops a chair with a loud bang whilst a dog is walking so that he is spooked, then give that exhibitor another opportunity to move his dog later on when he has had a chance to settle him. Make allowances too for young puppies which may be attending their first show, and be gentle and patient with them at all times.

The moment of decision comes only after every dog in a class has been assessed. If you have taken brief notes on individual dogs – a wise thing to do in large classes – now is the time to refer to them if you need to. Take your time at this point, thinking through what you are going to do, before calling the winners to the centre of the ring. Indicate clearly who is to come first, then second and so on, until the requisite number of winners are lined up awaiting their prizes. The dogs must be placed in descending order from the judge's left to his right before the judging book is marked up with the results. There is nothing worse than a display of indecision at this point, and we have all cringed when watching a judge call out three or four dogs into line only to change the second placed to third, then the fourth to second, and so on. I always have the placings completely clear in my mind before I call out the winners.

Ann Wynard looks over a class at Bournemouth Championship Show, 1993. (Photo: Audrey Dadds.)

Best of Breed is awarded after all the classes have been judged, at which time the steward will call into the ring all the dogs that have thus far remained unbeaten in their class. When there is an award for Best Puppy in Breed, it is as well to ask your steward to check in the catalogue that there were no puppies exhibited in classes other than

Judge Susan Johnson with her CC winners at Builth Wells, 1993. On the left is Vicki Grugan with Jardhu The Republican before he gained his title, to the right Sheila Richardson with Ch. Bellakerne Misty Do winning her twelfth CC. (Photo: Audrey Dadds.)

puppy, such as Novice. If there are any unbeaten puppies in later classes, then these too may be allowed to compete for the Best Puppy in Breed award together with the winners of puppy classes.

Writing Critiques

When a judge gets home after a show, sore of feet but hopefully basking in the sense of a job well done, there is one more task to be carried out. This is writing a report on the winners. The report, known as a critique, is sent to the canine press for publication amongst the show reports. Critique writing is a duty which every judge must undertake and which is owed to the exhibitors who entered the show. They will be watching out for the critique because they will want to see what the judge has to say about their dogs if they won, or to read about the dogs that beat them if they didn't get 'in the cards'. In addition, owners and breeders who were not able to get to the show will be waiting to read the critique.

Failure to write a critique for the dog papers is quite inexcusable, and there are many who wish to see critiques made a compulsory part of the judging contract. For a championship show, critiques are written on the dogs placed first and second in each class, whereas for any other sort of show a report on the first only is required.

There are pitfalls to avoid when writing critiques, such as praising a dog for a characteristic that is contrary to the Breed Standard or, conversely, criticizing a dog for a quality that the Breed Standard deems to be a virtue. Over the years I have made quite a collection of these – 'a lovely cobby little dog', for example (when of course the Shih Tzu is a breed in which cobbiness is a fault). Another pitfall is to write something that informed showgoers will know to be quite untrue. One judge wrote, 'just failed in dentition when it came to the decision for Best of Breed' about a dog which all of us who had judged it knew to have a full complement of perfectly placed teeth in a good wide jaw. Be sure of your facts before setting pen to paper.

Although it is not a hard and fast rule, there is a convention that too harsh a condemnation of a dog should not be written. If a judge slates a dog in a critique, people wonder why the exhibit was placed at all. If a winner, the best in the class on the day, failed in one respect (such as having a rather flat tail) then you might consider leaving out any mention of that part of the dog. The intelligent reader of critiques will spot this and know why you have done it. Matthew Prior, writing verse in the late seventeenth century, put it rather well when he wrote:

'Be to her virtues very kind,
Be to her faults a little blind.'

Although it was hardly what the poet intended, this seems to me a fairly sensible approach to critique writing.

Record Keeping

This subject usually provokes groans of protest from seminar audiences, yet it is essential for anyone who is embarking on a judging career to keep accurate and detailed records of all judging experience: a note of the date and name of the show, the breed or breeds judged, the number of classes, the number of dogs entered and the number of absentees. All this information should be kept in a safe place along with the judging book and a copy of the catalogue.

Other records that will come in useful later include a list of all litters of puppies bred, and the details of all Shih Tzus entered in the Kennel Club Stud Book (details should include each dog's Stud Book number). Also keep a diary of stewarding engagements, with details of the shows where these took place.

Awarding Challenge Certificates

The judge who has shown competence at open show level over a period of years can look forward to the day when an invitation to award Challenge Certificates plops onto the doormat for the first time. As with all other invitations to judge, it will come in the first instance from the society that is organizing the show, but will be followed in due course by a Kennel Club questionnaire. It is when you come to fill in the questionnaire that you will be so glad that you have kept meticulous records, because you will need all the details of your experience I have outlined above. On the basis of your answers, the appropriate Kennel Club committee will decide whether you are suitable to award CCs. The questionnaire provides an opportunity for a judge-elect to show details of additional qualifications, such as experience of judging breeds other than the one in question.

Int. Ch. Kelemar Linze-Lu, bred in 1986 by Ronnie and Margaret Brannick in England, and exported to Switzerland at six months by Walter Holtorf and Dieter Deppenmeier. Champion in Switzerland, Germany, Austria and Luxembourg, Top Shih Tzu 1988, and multi Best in Show winner. (Photo: David Dalton.)

To be suitably qualified in the eyes of the Kennel Club, a new judge at championship show level needs to have been successful in the show ring as an exhibitor or as a breeder, or both, and as a breed specialist is expected to have owned or bred at least three Shih Tzus that have won enough to be included in the stud book. A willingness to write critiques for the dog press must be declared, and evidence of a minimum of three years' experience as a steward must be shown. You must also have seven years or more experience of judging the breed. Given that the candidate is suitably qualified, the Kennel Club will usually give approval for the invitation to go through.

Judging Abroad

When it comes to judging abroad, the kennel clubs of many countries have a reciprocal agreement that only those who are approved to

Int. Ch. Gemihs Phoenix of Fire, top-winning Shih Tzu in Sweden in 1991, top-winning Shih Tzu Veteran in 1997. Bred by Gun-Marie Swedenhall, owned by Birgitta Jansson. (Photo: Gun-Marie Swedenhall.)

Fr. It. & Port. Ch. Baraka de Khadidja, Ch. du Monde 1992 and three times Best in Show, owned and bred by Jacqueline Bernard in France.

judge at championship show level in their own country are permitted to do so in another. Shih Tzu fanciers across the world are amazingly well informed about the strengths and weaknesses of the breed in each other's countries, and when you judge abroad you usually do so in front of a very knowlegeable and sophisticated audience. Each country has its own rules of procedure, so if you are invited to officiate in a foreign country, make yourself completely familiar with how things are done there. You must also find out if there is a different Breed Standard.

It is a wonderful experience to judge abroad, to meet new devotees of the breed, see different Shih Tzus and make new friends, but it is hard work too. Anyone who judges overseas acts as an ambassador for his or her own country and should behave accordingly. In Sweden and some other countries, each dog is individually graded and has its own critique, and judges who are unaccustomed to this may find it rather daunting. If possible it is better to have visited dog shows overseas as a spectator first, rather than attempt to take on the task of judging without a clear idea of what is involved.

9

Breeding

The process of breeding is a matter of bringing together the genes of the male dog with those of the female, selecting the best out of the resulting puppies, and then repeating the process in the next generation. The purpose is to produce dogs that match ever more closely the ideal described in the Breed Standard, as well as having good physical and mental health. The hereditary characteristics of the puppy, in both physical appearance and character, are determined by the genes inherited from the parents for each characteristic, one gene is donated by the sire and the other by the dam. The problem is that there are so many genes, more than 25,000 strung like beads on each chromosome, and thirty-nine pairs of chromosomes per dog, that the permutations by which they may be rearranged in the next generation are pretty well infinite.

Fortunately, breeding dogs does not require an expert knowledge of genetics. Were it so, I and a good many others might never have been able to plan for, await with a mixture of anticipation and apprehension, and finally exult in the arrival of a litter of puppies. However, since dog breeding is just as subject to the laws of genetics as the breeding of any other species, a little understanding of the basic

Jardhu Lotus Blossom, looking very grown up at nine months. (Photo: Alan Walker.)

principles can be a great help. I am not qualified to do more than offer a brief introduction, but there are plenty of good books on the subject for those who are interested in learning more (*see* Further Reading).

In practical terms, there are three options open to the breeder: inbreeding, line-breeding and outcrossing. Each has its advantages and pitfalls. The route taken at any one time will depend largely on experience and awareness of pedigrees, not just as lists of names but through knowledge of the dogs therein, and that elusive quality, 'an eye for a good dog'.

Inbreeding

This is the mating of two dogs that are very closely related indeed, such as father to daughter or brother to sister. It is sometimes frowned on and with good reason, although it is a method by which two exceptionally sound dogs could be brought together by an experienced and knowledgeable breeder to double up on all their virtues. The danger is that hitherto hidden faults may also appear, and the practice has even been known to result in a litter of puppies that has had to be destroyed. Certainly it would be very unwise for a novice to take this path, because inbreeding fixes not only good points but also bad, and therefore requires a detailed knowledge of the ancestors in the pedigree of both dog and bitch.

Line-breeding

Experience has shown that this is a successful way to go about breeding, and so it is quite commonly used. To line-breed is to choose a stud dog that is related to the bitch through having at least one ancestor in common: examples of this sort of mating might be uncle to niece, grandfather to granddaughter or a mating between cousins. Each time such a mating is carried out, the puppies will receive some of the same genes from each of their parents, and this will obviously help to preserve and fix the characteristics these genes are governing. Like inbreeding, this course of action requires knowledge of the ancestors of both dog and bitch, and especially of the ancestor that is going to appear twice or perhaps more often in the pedigree of the pups. The advantage of this method over that of inbreeding is that it allows one to proceed cautiously, step by step, and to change direction as soon as an undesirable development occurs. Over the years, I have seen some of the most successful British breeders pursue a policy of line-breeding for several generations, followed by one carefully chosen outcross and then a cross back into the maternal line. The most successful of all have been those who, free from prejudice and kennel blindness, have also known when to change direction because things have started to go wrong.

Outcrossing

Outcrossing is sometimes described as the mating of unrelated dogs, and is somewhat difficult when it comes to the Shih Tzu because all the present-day stock is descended from the same small group of imported animals (*see* Chapter 1). For our purposes, outcrossing can better be regarded as the mating of dogs that are not related closely, as for example when there are no common ancestors on a five-genera-tion pedigree. Using this approach, the breeder may choose a stud dog purely on his appearance, or because of the appearance of the dogs he has previously sired. In a way this is a bit like doing the lot-tery, albeit with better odds, because the genetic make-up of the dog is being ignored, but this is not to condemn the idea out of hand. The chances of success are greatly increased if either or both of the dogs concerned are line-bred, and this is also a method that has proved successful in the past.

The Brood Bitch

Let us first dispose of the fanciful notion that a bitch, any bitch even if she was purchased specifically as a pet, should be allowed to have just one litter because 'it's good for her'. The pet bitch is perfectly happy with her human family and it is better for her to be spayed at a suitable age than to have pregnancy inflicted upon her by someone who, while claiming to love her, has neither the equipment nor the experience to help her through it. If a Shih Tzu is intended as a mother-to-be, she should have been bought with that in mind. She should be a sound and typical specimen of the breed, and she must have been maintained in excellent condition throughout her puppy-hood and young maturity, because a poorly reared bitch, overweight and under-exercised, is never going to make the best of mothers.

Although a bitch is capable of conception in her first season, which usually occurs when she is about six months old, this must never be allowed to happen. At that age she is but a puppy herself and has not finished growing physically nor developing mentally. Shih Tzus have quite an extended puppyhood compared with some other breeds, and it is a shame to deprive them of this most enjoyable period of their young lives. There are Kennel Club rules and regulations about the age at which a bitch may be mated, and most breed clubs also apply restrictions through the codes of ethics by which members agree to abide as a condition of joining. After the first season, a Shih Tzu bitch may follow a regular pattern and come into season every six months, or she may have a longer interval between seasons. It is not all that uncommon for a bitch to come into season only once a year, but wild variations in the length of time between seasons may be worth investigating in case they indicate an infection or some sort of hormonal problem.

Before making the decision to have a litter with your maiden bitch, it is a good idea to take her to your veterinary surgeon for a thorough physical check, part of which will be an examination to make sure that there is no obstruction to prevent mating taking place. If there is time, try to have a chat about the whole procedure, because the vet is going to be your best friend if you have any problems during pregnancy or whelping, and will have some general advice that is well worth listening to. The Shih Tzu has long been regarded as an easy whelping breed, and by taking these precautions it will help to keep it so. Check that the bitch's vaccinations are all up to date, and that she has been wormed before the time comes to mate her.

The Stud Dog

Management of the Stud Dog

A stud dog is a special type of male Shih Tzu, not just the nearest and most convenient, nor the latest top winner. Ideally, he is an exceptionally sound, healthy and typical specimen of the breed, of show-winning appearance and with a good ancestry. He is of even more value as a stud if he is also found to be prepotent, producing offspring that carry his good qualities when he is mated to a variety of differently bred bitches. It should go without saying that he must also be of prodigiously good temperament, but I fear this is sometimes overlooked by those breeding predominantly for show points. A dog with an undescended testicle should not offered at stud, for he is likely to produce monorchid or cryptorchid dogs, or possibly dogs and bitches that carry the gene for this abnormality and can thus pass it on to their own progeny in the next generation.

A young dog should not start at stud before the age of about ten months, with no more than one further mating before the age of a year and at the most another two before reaching eighteen months old. He will do very well with less, but ought not to mate too many bitches at a stage of his life when he still has some growing to do. In the wild, there would be long periods of rest for any dog, and a youngster would be very unlikely to achieve a position within the pack order such that he would get any chance at mating the bitches, this being the prerogative of the pack leader. Overuse of a popular stud dog can cause temporary or even permanent infertility, besides which there is an increased danger of bacterial infection being transferred from bitch to bitch if he serves two or more within a short period.

The owner of a stud dog has many responsibilities beyond the acceptance of the stud fees. I believe that he or she has a duty to permit a mating only if reasonably satisfied that the alliance has a good chance of producing sound and typical progeny, and that the resulting puppies will be properly reared and sold only to suitable homes. However, I know that my views are regarded as extreme in some quarters, and that some owners maintain they are paid merely for the dog's services and not to police every possible contingency thereafter. The dog must be maintained in first-class condition, fed with a good diet, regularly vaccinated and periodically tested to establish that he is free from infections. The owner should also be quite clear about the terms at which the dog's services are offered, and put these in writing.

Infertility in a male Shih Tzu may, as already mentioned, result from overuse, but it can also be caused by a lot of other factors, including congenital ones about which nothing can be done, disease or even poor diet. Sometimes a dog fails to mate in the first place, and there are two main reasons for this. When he is keen to mate but cannot achieve it, there may be a physical deformity of the penis, or pain resulting from a penile infection. In this sort of situation a veterinary examination is advised to try to find the root of the trouble. A second reason for a dog not to mate a bitch is that he is unwilling: he just doesn't want to. This could be a rare case of impotence from hormonal imbalance but is more likely due to psychological reasons. The latter could be caused by his owner having checked his sexual behaviour as a pup, as I know to my cost, keeping my Shih Tzus as I do in a family situation. In more than one case where I have said, 'Don't *do* that,' just once too often to a keen young male making advances to one of our bitches, and where the same dog has grown up to become particularly bonded to me, the outcome has been that he simply won't attempt to mate a bitch in my presence – my own fault, of course, although other dogs have been far less sensitive to my feelings on the matter!

When you consult your vet about infertility problems, the best treatment will be more easily determined if you can provide detailed notes based on observation of the dog's history, symptoms and behaviour, to complement the physical examination. As with so many other aspects of dog care, the vet/breeder relationship should be an interactive partnership.

Choosing a Dog

A breeder – by definition the owner of the bitch – is in the fortunate position of having a huge choice when it comes to picking a dog to sire a litter of puppies. There will be many males available at stud up and down the land, but it is not always easy to make the correct choice. Suppose that we have a bitch from whom we want to have a litter of puppies: she is quite a good example of the breed, or we would not be thinking of mating her, but she is very leggy, a fault we would like to eliminate. You might think that you need a short-legged husband for her, on the principle that the puppies will have a leg-length somewhere in between. Mixing genes is not as simple as mixing paint, however, and a likely result would be that some puppies would be tall like their dam, whilst others would have excessively short legs like their sire.

What we should do with our leggy bitch is to mate her to a male of good quality with exactly the right length of leg, selecting from the puppies the best one of those that resemble the father in length of leg to retain for future breeding. Problem solved? Not necessarily, for in each of the pairs of genes that govern leg length the puppy will have inherited one gene from each parent. You know that one of this pair of genes dictates correct length of leg because he visibly possesses this trait. But it is likely that the other gene in the pair, inherited from his mother, will be the gene for legginess, which he may then pass on to his children and grandchildren, in whom it may manifest itself.

This example, is of course, a gross oversimplification, but I hope it is perhaps enough to make it understandable why so many people have been tempted to give up on the theory of genetics and simply 'mate the best to the best and hope for the best'. However, even a very basic understanding of what is happening has enabled us to choose the second dog in the example given as a much better mate for our hypothetical bitch. So far, we have considered only the appearance (or phenotype) of the stud dog, but if we then consider his pedigree (or genotype) this enables us to see that if the dog is himself closely line-bred he will be able to have a better influence on the puppies, and also that if the ancestor to which he is line-bred is known to excel in the virtue we are looking for this will again increase our chances of success.

One of the pitfalls to avoid when choosing a stud dog is that of rushing off to use the latest champion without considering if his pedigree merits this decision, or if he is a producer of good-quality puppies. Indeed, if such a champion, or any other dog for that matter, particularly appeals to the breeder it is probably a good idea to look at the possibility of using his father at stud. The experienced breeder sees the qualities and the faults in a stud dog in the light of all his ancestors for many generations back and evaluates them accordingly. Another pitfall is that of using the dog 'up the road' or your own dog for reasons of convenience. This can be just as bad a mistake, as either may be unsuitable for the bitch that is to be mated, in terms of pedigree and appearance.

One thing that is just as important as genotype or phenotype is the matter of temperament, something which is sometimes given insufficient consideration by breeders in their planning. Never mind that you breed the most beautiful Shih Tzus imaginable, you will still have done our breed a great disservice if these dogs lack the correct temperament, if they are timid or snappy or worse. Of course, it is not always easy to be sure of the chosen stud dog's temperament, since you do not own him, but by keeping your eyes and ears open it is often possible to find out about any failings in this respect. A stud dog of uncertain temper should be avoided at all costs.

Planning a Litter

Planning for a litter is important, and includes not only the choice of the sire for your new Shih Tzu family, but also every possible detail of the care of the bitch during pregnancy, the time and the place of whelping, and the all-important aftercare of the mother and her family. This may sound too obvious to need stating, but I have actually known of one family who mated their bitch without doing the arithmetic that would have caused them to realise that they would be away at about the time of her whelping, and this stupid mistake cost them quite a lot of money when they cancelled their travel plans. Taking into account the latter stages of pregnancy and the key weeks of a litter's development, times during which someone will need to be available to attend to the needs of the mother and her family, I would say that there will be a period of up to eighteen weeks during which a breeder can expect to be pretty well tied to home. A litter of puppies is the most time-consuming thing I know: apart from the constant care they need, I find that I spend hours and hours just watching them, and playing with them as they grow older. I have also had the heartbreaking experience of nursing and caring for a tiny puppy, only to see it die despite all my efforts.

As with most things in life there will be financial considerations to take into account, apart from the stud fee. Even if everything goes perfectly, so that there are no charges for veterinary attendance to pay for, the cost of feeding a pregnant bitch for nine weeks and afterwards having a litter of puppies to feed until they finally go to good homes can mount up to a lot of money. And then if things do go wrong, as when a Caesarean section is required for example, expenses can escalate at a frightening rate. Anyone who has groaned at the cost of having routine annual vaccinations for one dog can calculate the damage when a litter of six puppies all need to be vaccinated, and this is an expense which will fall upon the breeder if the puppies do not leave for their new homes before vaccinations become due.

It is the breeder's job, having made the choice of a stud, to approach his owner for permission to use the dog, remembering that not all dogs are available for use at public stud. Once the use of the stud dog has been agreed, it is advisable to agree all the terms in advance so that there will be no arguments later on. Then it is a case of waiting until the bitch next comes into season.

The Season

Keeping records of your bitch's seasons is always worth while, since it is necessary to keep her safe from accidental matings at such times.

These records prove particularly useful when you are planning a mating, as they enable the breeder to watch more accurately for the onset of the season and to advise the stud dog owner of the likely schedule. A typical season lasts approximately three weeks, counting from the first signs, which are bleeding (a sign that can easily be missed if the bitch keeps herself very clean) and a very obvious swelling of the vulva. The first stage of the season lasts about a week, during which she will on no account stand to receive a male although she may be coy and flirty with the other bitches in the household.

The second stage is marked by a softening of the vulva, whilst at the same time the colour of the vaginal discharge changes to a lighter, almost translucent colour, and continues until somewhere during the third week of the season, when the process draws to a close and everything returns to normal. It is somewhere during the second stage that mating can take place. Occasionally a bitch can have what is known as a 'silent' season, when no blood-coloured discharge is seen at all. This sort of season can easily be missed altogether, unless there is a male Shih Tzu somewhere around in which case he will undoubtedly have noticed what is going on.

When to Mate

The stud dog owner should be notified as soon as the bitch's season has begun, but it is not possible at that stage to make a firm arrangement for the day of mating as this varies so much from bitch to bitch. It is vital to pick the right day for the mating because choosing the wrong time is a common reason for failure to get the bitch into whelp. The owner of one lovely Shih Tzu male, much used at stud, told me wryly that she was always amazed at how many bitches conveniently reached the point of mating at the weekend (according to their owners), but that if any matings were going to miss it was usually these.

Signs of readiness to be mated include the bitch swinging her tail sharply to one side, standing braced if you press lightly on her rear end, or perhaps mounting other Shih Tzus in the household. All or some of these will occur together with the softening of the vulva and lessening of colour in the vaginal discharge which I have already mentioned. It is generally found that bitches will be ready to mate somewhere between the eleventh and fourteenth days, but this is by no means a hard and fast rule, as I found out a few years ago.

I had agreed to have one of my dogs used to mate a friend's maiden bitch, and when the bitch was in season and showing signs of readiness they were duly mated, this being on about the eleventh or twelfth day. No puppies were produced, and with the wisdom of hindsight we decided that perhaps we had tried a touch early. On her next season we tried again, but this time on about the thirteenth to fourteenth day, achieving what we thought was a really good mating. There were no puppies this time either. By now, I was beginning to suggest my friend should try another stud dog – after all, I pointed out, my lad was not exactly in the first flush of youth. However, my friend was made of sterner stuff and, determined to use the dog she wanted, she opted for a third try, but this time invested in an ovulation test. The test told us to mate the bitch on the seventeenth day, and this we duly did although she was by this time only just willing to stand for the dog (old chum though he had by now become), and even he was at first only lukewarm. The result of this third mating was six puppies. I am not suggesting that going to the trouble and expense of an ovulation test should ever be necessary as a routine procedure, but it is certainly worth considering should it prove difficult to get a bitch into whelp.

The Mating

British breeders are luckier than those in some other countries, in that it is rarely if ever necessary to send Shih Tzus off by train or plane to be mated. The distances involved are usually such that we can avoid that sort of trauma for our bitches by taking them to the stud dog ourselves, and this is normally done by car. It is wisest not to feed the bitch before the journey, and upon arrival to let her relieve herself and gain a little familiarity with her surroundings before she is introduced to the male. If the stud dog is experienced, and likewise if his owners know what they are about, the actual mating should be achieved without any problems even if the bitch is a maiden. The worst situation is when both stud dog and bitch are inexperienced, with owners who are new to the game too. If this should happen to be the case I would strongly recommend that a breeder with a bit more knowledge should be called in to assist and advise. If the people who are supervising a mating are clumsy or nervous this will be picked up at once by the dogs, and may even inhibit their mating instincts, especially in the case with a bitch that is particularly bonded with her owner. Keep calm, and avoid having an audience for the mating procedure.

Shih Tzu stud dogs vary in their approach to a bitch. Some will make a businesslike approach and immediately mount her, clasping their forelegs firmly round her loin. Others will prefer to do a little courting first: years ago I had a dog whose idea of foreplay included a vast amount of ear licking preceded by a little dance. He always performed this dance first, oblivious to the look of disdain which some bitches used to give him. One Shih Tzu breeder has her 'mating mat', a small piece of carpet which prevents the dog's feet from slipping as he mounts the bitch; all her stud dogs know what the mat is for, and the excitement when it is produced is very amusing to watch. If the dog is having difficulty in finding his target, it is possible to guide him by slipping a hand under the bitch's tummy from the side and placing a finger to each side of the vulva so that you can detect whether she is positioned correctly, gently adjusting her stance if necessary. If the dog is not tall enough, put something under his feet to raise him up a bit. This sort of assistance is only possible if the stud dog is willing to accept his owner's intervention, and I hope it is not necessary to stress that assistance should never go as far as attempting to force the mating if either dog or bitch is genuinely unwilling.

After the dog has penetrated the bitch, a 'bulb' at the base of his penis swells up and the vaginal muscles contract in response: this is called the 'tie' because it effectively prevents the mating pair from separating. I particularly mention it because I once heard of a pair of novice breeders attempting to pull the pair apart under the impression that they had 'just got stuck somehow'. The tie can last anything from a couple of minutes up to as much as an hour, but the length of the tie does not bear any relation to the success of the mating in terms of producing puppies; indeed, it is perfectly possible for a bitch to conceive in the case of a 'slip' mating, one where no tie has taken place at all.

Sometimes the dog will remain on the bitch's back whilst tied, but often he will show an inclination to move his front legs off, lift one hind leg over her back and turn so that they are standing back to back: the stud dog owner will gently assist in this process if necessary, thereafter steadying the dog while the owner of the bitch holds her head to prevent her trying to pull away.

After the tie is released, the dog will ease away from the bitch, and should be put somewhere quiet to relax for a while. Later, his owner should check that the penis has withdrawn into its sheath, because with a long-coated dog like the Shih Tzu it is possible for some hair to become caught up and this is very uncomfortable for the dog.

Although some breeders tell me they never have any problems, I always avoid reintroducing the stud dog at once to his male companions because of the jealousy this can cause. Instead, I rest him and then give him a rinse underneath with a mild antibacterial solution before he goes back to boast of his exploits to his chums. After mating, the bitch too should be given a time of rest. Later, she will probably like to have a drink of water and relieve herself before the journey home.

Some breeders prefer to arrange multiple matings, at least two often being preferred, usually within forty-eight hours of each other, although if the first mating was satisfactory a second should not really be necessary. However, if two matings are acceptable to both breeder and stud dog owner there is certainly no harm in this, and if it is felt that perhaps the bitch was only just ready the first time then a second mating may be a good idea. All such contingencies should be discussed before the day of the mating comes, so that arrangements can be made by both parties. The stud fee should be paid at the time of the mating, and indeed the mating (rather than conception) is what the fee is for, although many stud dog owners are quite generous in offering to provide another mating to the same bitch or even to another if no puppies are produced. One occasion when a fee may not be asked for until conception is confirmed is when the stud dog is not proved, which is to say that he has not yet sired progeny.

Less commonly, a stud dog owner will sometimes offer to take a puppy from the resulting litter, possibly the pick of the litter, instead of charging a fee. This may seem tempting, but I do think it best to avoid such an arrangement if possible, and I say this for two reasons. You will surely wish to have first choice of your puppies for yourself, assuming that your motive in breeding is to acquire the next generation of your own Shih Tzu family rather than breeding to sell for short-term profit. Secondly, anyone who is tempted to offer a puppy instead of a fee because of financial difficulties should not really be contemplating breeding at all, because as I have already pointed out the fee is just the first of many expenses, and you must be prepared to budget for all of these.

10

Pregnancy and Whelping

Nine weeks to go: the average length of a bitch's gestation period is exactly sixty-three days, although it is not at all unusual for the puppies to arrive three or four days early, and they can appear up to a week early without any real problems. However, puppies that are born more than a week prematurely have a much-reduced chance of survival. Occasionally, whelping does not start until a day or so after the sixty-third day, but this is less normal. To save all that mental arithmetic, a chart is provided, showing the normal gestation period from each day in the year (*see* page 157).

The nine weeks of pregnancy are best considered in three sections.

The First Three Weeks

This is really just the 'wait and see' time, because there is no reliable way of telling if you have puppies on the way or not at this stage. The bitch will behave much as she usually does, with no physical changes nor any indications of a different attitude to life, so treat her exactly as normal, feeding and exercising as usual. A word about diet: in the old days, we used to add a full complement of mineral and vitamin supplements to the bitch's food throughout her pregnancy, and usually provided extra calcium in the belief that this would guard against eclampsia. However, such supplements are no longer recommended because modern complete foods are carefully formulated to contain all the nutrients necessary for health. In addition, some vets now tell us that too much calcium can have a detrimental effect on growth and specifically on bone development. In view of this, it is a good idea to consult your vet before putting any additives into the food of the in-whelp bitch. During the first stage of pregnancy, as at any other time of life, it is important that the bitch is kept fit and healthy, neither too fat nor too thin. A sensible feeding regime using top-quality food is the key, combined with sensible exercise.

The Second Three Weeks

From the twenty-first day through the fourth week of pregnancy, your vet will be able to feel the presence of puppies. A week or so later there will be more fluid in the uterus but the puppies will not yet have grown much, and so it may not be possible to determine if there are whelps there at all. Such is the conformation of the Shih Tzu that some bitches, particularly maiden ones, carry their puppies tucked up high under the rib cage, and so, even if an expert is unable to feel them, there may still be one or two present. Some people like to take a bitch for scanning at this period: this is a process by which an experienced operator can see whether there are puppies present, and even indicate how many are there. I do not feel the need to go to such lengths to find out whether my bitch is pregnant or not – after all, this is going to become clear quite soon anyway – but for some breeders it can be very useful to have the pregnancy confirmed early. The scanning procedure seems to be perfectly safe. However, even if whelps are detected it is possible for them to be absorbed at a later stage.

During this second stage, there are signs of pregnancy which the observant breeder will be able to spot. One is a change in behaviour, as when a usually extrovert bitch becomes rather quiet and clingy, or vice versa. Sometimes the teats will appear to be more prominent and a more definite pink colour than usual. Another sign may be a change in eating habits, with a greedy bitch going off her food for a few days or becoming excessively fussy about what she eats, or one that is not normally greedy refusing to eat at all. It can be exasperating that a bitch should go off her food just when one is so anxious that she should be eating well, but this is quite common and usually lasts only a short time. If she is off her food for a week or more, you will need to try to get her eating again. Usually, a finicky eater can be tempted with something a bit special or highly flavoured: I have found that such delicacies as roast chicken, sliced cooked sausage or sardines have worked in such circumstances!

There is no need to increase the food intake too much during the second stage of pregnancy, although the mother-to-be may take a little more than previously. A healthy bitch will be happy to continue to take routine exercise and will be all the fitter for having plenty of activity. I always try to discourage any leaping about and jumping on chairs from this stage on. The puppies will not start to gain weight really fast until weeks seven to nine, so the bitch should not yet appear to be obese and too heavy.

The Last Three Weeks

Now, during weeks seven to nine, things really start to happen. The puppies make up to two-thirds of their total growth during this time, so the bitch starts to thicken and she will also need more food, although it may be that she will be reluctant to eat much because she will be feeling uncomfortable. It is a good idea to feed two or even three small meals rather than one large one, and increase the protein content of the meals. I have often found that my pregnant bitches will take an egg for breakfast, hard-boiled or scrambled, but in either case the egg must always be cooked very thoroughly indeed. One of the things to watch for at this stage is constipation: I have found a small dose of liquid paraffin can help with this. Give only a teaspoon and this only once or twice, because repeated dosage with liquid paraffin is said to inhibit the intake of vitamins.

I like to give my pregnant bitch a bath during the seventh or eighth week, as later she may grow too heavy and uncomfortable for this sort of attention. At the same time, I carefully trim off all the long hair around the tummy and the teats, but have not normally found it necessary to cut the rest of the coat short, as it can be tied up into bunches

Sometimes a breeder will prefer to cut off the long coat when a bitch is nursing puppies.

Whelping chart.

Jan	Mar	Feb	Apr	Mar	May	Apr	Jun	May	Jul	Jun	Aug	Jul	Sep	Aug	Oct	Sep	Nov	Oct	Dec	Nov	Jan	Dec	Feb
1	5	1	5	1	3	1	3	1	3	1	3	1	2	1	3	1	3	1	3	1	3	1	2
2	6	2	6	2	4	2	4	2	4	2	4	2	3	2	4	2	4	2	4	2	4	2	3
3	7	3	7	3	5	3	5	3	5	3	5	3	4	3	5	3	5	3	5	3	5	3	4
4	8	4	8	4	6	4	6	4	6	4	6	4	5	4	6	4	6	4	6	4	6	4	5
5	9	5	9	5	7	5	7	5	7	5	7	5	6	5	7	5	7	5	7	5	7	5	6
6	10	6	10	6	8	6	8	6	8	6	8	6	7	6	8	6	8	6	8	6	8	6	7
7	11	7	11	7	9	7	9	7	9	7	9	7	8	7	9	7	9	7	9	7	9	7	8
8	12	8	12	8	10	8	10	8	10	8	10	8	9	8	10	8	10	8	10	8	10	8	9
9	13	9	13	9	11	9	11	9	11	9	11	9	10	9	11	9	11	9	11	9	11	9	10
10	14	10	14	10	12	10	12	10	12	10	12	10	11	10	12	10	12	10	12	10	12	10	11
11	15	11	15	11	13	11	13	11	13	11	13	11	12	11	13	11	13	11	13	11	13	11	12
12	16	12	16	12	14	12	14	12	14	12	14	12	13	12	14	12	14	12	14	12	14	12	13
13	17	13	17	13	15	13	15	13	15	13	15	13	14	13	15	13	15	13	15	13	15	13	14
14	18	14	18	14	16	14	16	14	16	14	16	14	15	14	16	14	16	14	16	14	16	14	15
15	19	15	19	15	17	15	17	15	17	15	17	15	16	15	17	15	17	15	17	15	17	15	16
16	20	16	20	16	18	16	18	16	18	16	18	16	17	16	18	16	18	16	18	16	18	16	17
17	21	17	21	17	19	17	19	17	19	17	19	17	18	17	19	17	19	17	19	17	19	17	18
18	22	18	22	18	20	18	20	18	20	18	20	18	19	18	20	18	20	18	20	18	20	18	19
19	23	19	23	19	21	19	21	19	21	19	21	19	20	19	21	19	21	19	21	19	21	19	20
20	24	20	24	20	22	20	22	20	22	20	22	20	21	20	22	20	22	20	22	20	22	20	21
21	25	21	25	21	23	21	23	21	23	21	23	21	22	21	23	21	23	21	23	21	23	21	22
22	26	22	26	22	24	22	24	22	24	22	24	22	23	22	24	22	24	22	24	22	24	22	23
23	27	23	27	23	25	23	25	23	25	23	25	23	24	23	25	23	25	23	25	23	25	23	24
24	28	24	28	24	26	24	26	24	26	24	26	24	25	24	26	24	26	24	26	24	26	24	25
25	29	25	29	25	27	25	27	25	27	25	27	25	26	25	27	25	27	25	27	25	27	25	26
26	30	26	30	26	28	26	28	26	28	26	28	26	27	26	28	26	28	26	28	26	28	26	27
27	31	27	May 1	27	29	27	29	27	29	27	29	27	28	27	29	27	29	27	29	27	29	27	28
28	Apr 1	28	May 2	28	30	28	30	28	30	28	30	28	29	28	30	28	30	28	30	28	30	28	Mar 1
29	Apr 2			29	31	29	Jul 1	29	31	29	31	29	30	29	31	29	Dec 1	29	31	29	31	29	Mar 2
30	Apr 3			30	Jun 1	30	Jul 2	30	Aug 1	30	Sep 1	30	Oct 1	30	Nov 1	30	Dec 2	30	Jan 1	30	Feb 1	30	Mar 3
31	Apr 4			31	Jun 2			31	Aug 2			31	Oct 2	31	Nov 2			31	Jan 2			31	Mar 4

Whelping chart. The first figure in each column indicates mating date, the second the expected whelping date.

157

to keep it out of the way during whelping. Some breeders like to plait the long hair on the body and the tail during and after the birth of the puppies, but I have never got on with this method and have found that it seemed to cause the hair to mat worse than if I had left it free.

As she grows heavier, the bitch may of her own accord give up leaping on and off chairs, or scampering up and down stairs. This is not always so and you have to be vigilant that she does not overdo it. One of the delights of the last week of pregnancy is that, when the bitch is lying quietly at your side, it is possible to feel the fluttering movements of the new life within by laying your fingers gently along her flank.

The ninth week of pregnancy is not a time to leave a bitch unattended for very long, as the birth process may start at any time and is quite likely to take place three to five days ahead of schedule. This should not cause any problems, so long as everything is fully prepared and the mother-to-be is not left alone for any length of time. One hears stories of Shih Tzu bitches who have got on with it and produced their puppies without any help at all, but equally there are sad accounts of the mother failing to break open the membranous sac and being unable to bite the cord because of her short face. Indeed, a maiden bitch may be frightened and confused, and not be sure what to do at all. It is simply not worth taking the risk.

During these last weeks it is a good idea to introduce the bitch to her whelping quarters, with the whelping box in place, although Shih Tzus can on occasion be rather awkward about the breeder's choice of where to have the puppies because they tend to have ideas of their own. I never bother to make an issue of this, as once the actual birth starts the bitch will be too busy to make a fuss about where she is placed. Meanwhile she should not be stressed, so it is better to let her investigate all the odd corners of the house if she really wants to. Choose somewhere quiet for the whelping, out of the way of family traffic, because it is essential for the bitch to feel happy and secure both before and after giving birth.

The False Pregnancy

The most experienced breeders have been fooled from time to time by this phenomenon, because a bitch can display all the right signs, growing larger and larger and even producing milk in the final stages, all for nothing. It is very disappointing when this happens. It can also be very upsetting for a bitch, because she believes that she is going to produce puppies and when none appear she can become extremely unsettled and depressed, as well as being very uncomfortable if she is producing a lot of milk. In extreme cases, I have known Shih Tzus who have nested, gone through a period almost like whelping itself and then become morbidly attached to some of their toys, which they carry about and lick and mother, almost to distraction.

Apart from giving medication to reduce the amount of milk, the best way to help a bitch with a false pregnancy is to try to distract her from her condition. It is a mistake to treat her like an invalid: it is much better to take her for walks, play with her as much as possible and in general keep her mind off the problem. I have found that a bitch with one false pregnancy to her credit will tend to have another and then another, in which case it is often kinder to have her spayed in order to spare her this sort of trauma every six months or so.

Preparations for Whelping

I have sometimes been amazed to hear breeders reeling off the list of things they feel that they must have to hand when a bitch is to whelp: frankly, I wouldn't know what to do with some of the equipment which others regard as essential! The best equipment of all is the ability to keep calm under pressure and a sure instinct for when it is necessary to panic and call the vet. Both of these can be borrowed if you are lucky enough to have an experienced Shih Tzu breeder standing by to come to your aid for your very first litter of puppies.

The minimum requirements are:

Newspapers
Towels   Find large ones, and also cut an old one up into small squares that can be used to hold a newborn puppy securely if required.
Mild disinfectant   I buy mine in a spray bottle, for quick application to the hands.
Paper tissues
A bin with lid   For waste material.
Veterinary thermometer
Petroleum jelly   To put on the thermometer before use.
Sterilized scissors
Hot-water bottle and soft blanket   Put the hot-water bottle in the bottom of a small cardboard box into which it fits snugly, and fold the

soft blanket on top. This will serve as a temporary nest for the first puppies whilst the later ones are being delivered, and will also come in useful if you need to rush the new family off to the vet.

Scales   For weighing puppies.

Notepaper   To keep a record of events as they occur, and of puppy weights.

Heat source   Heated pad or heated whelping bed.

Brandy   For resuscitating puppies (not for the breeder!).

Whelping box

The whelping box can be a purpose-built and quite costly piece of equipment or a very simple home-made box. The basic requirements are the same: it must be easy to keep scrupulously clean, free from draughts, and large enough for the bitch to lie stretched out at the side of her babies without being so large that a puppy can become isolated from the warmth of its litter-mates and mother. There must also be flap at the front to prevent the puppies from rolling or crawling out. Many breeders like to have a rail round the inner sides of the box, about 2–3in (5–7.5cm) above the base and sticking out a couple of inches from the side, the purpose of which is to prevent the mother from lying on her puppies.

The whelping box (occupied to indicate the required size), with a protective rail. The box will be lined with suitable bedding material (see page 161).

My choice is to have two whelping boxes. The first is an open bed, with rigid sides for the bitch to push against if she wishes. It is much easier for me to attend to her than it would be in an enclosed box. I line the bed with flat newspapers, fix a cotton sheet flat on top, and on top of that put a plentiful supply of small loose towels for her to scratch up as she wishes. When all the puppies have arrived, I transfer mother and family to the second bed, which I have prepared in advance. This is about 30in by 24in (76cm by 60cm), and has a heating pad over half of the base, leaving the other half unheated for the mother to move to if she is feeling too hot. The base is covered with fleecy material obtainable for the purpose from pet shops or something similar. This second bed has no sides, but I provide these cheaply enough by begging from a local store a large cardboard box (the sort in which washing machines are delivered). This I cut to shape, leaving a low lip at the front and making the top into a flap which can be lifted or lowered as needed. The bed stands inside this cardboard box, and then when the puppies have grown the box is discarded, so there is never any question of infection going from one litter to the next. There is no door at the front of my improvised whelping boxes since I never shut a bitch in with her family but leave her free to come and go as she chooses. I sometimes hang a towel over the front when I want to exclude drafts or to maintain the humidity of the interior of the box.

Signs of Approaching Whelping

Detecting when labour is beginning may be difficult for the inexperienced breeder, because the bitch can show signs of restlessness for some time before peacefully going to sleep just when it seems that something must be up. She may start 'nesting' or bedmaking and then stop again, and all this can be quite nerve-racking for the owner who is not prepared for it. However, there is one more reliable sign that whelping is not far off, and that is a change in her temperature. The normal temperature of 101.4°F (39°C) will drop to somewhere around 98°F (36°C) in the day or so before whelping, so if a bitch has a normal temperature it is not likely that she is going to whelp within the next twelve hours. Take her temperature daily during the ninth week of pregnancy to be sure of spotting when the tell-tale drop occurs.

Usually a bitch will refuse to eat once the birth process is starting. She will be restless, as mentioned above, and also tend to pant and shiver, sometimes turning sharply towards her rear, perhaps scratching up her bedding frantically meanwhile. These signs may last for a few hours or much longer, and it is during this stage that the birth passages are dilating ready for the birth. This is not a process that can be hurried, and it is the breeder's job to wait and watch calmly, displaying no outward signs of anxiety that could be picked up by the bitch, but being always alert for the first contraction.

The Normal Birth

The first contraction is much easier to recognize than most novices anticipate. It is marked by a strong and rhythmical straining movement, and the time when this is first seen must be carefully noted down. Contractions will occur with increasing frequency up to the time the water bag containing the first puppy appears in the vulva. The bag may retreat and then reappear at the next contraction, it may break and release the fluid within, or it may not break until after the head appears, in which case it must be torn open at once so that the puppy may breathe. After the birth the placenta should follow at the next contraction, still attached to the puppy by the umbilical cord.

Although it is normal for a bitch to attend to the severing of the umbilical cord herself, the Shih Tzu is not very well equipped to do this because of the shortness of her foreface and the fact that she may have an undershot jaw, so it is best if the breeder lends a hand at this point. The cord can be short, so that the newborn whelp is held close to the vulva, and it can be quite tough too; despite this it is better to tear it than to cut it because the latter is more likely to cause bleeding. Take the cord firmly between finger and thumb and squeeze it with a milking action towards the puppy once or twice before tearing it apart. This method causes little loss of blood and obviates the need to tie or clamp the cord. Place the puppy at once onto a nipple to get it sucking away, while its mother will want to lick vigorously at her offspring. Some bitches show a desire to eat the placenta, but this is not essential and I would not advise giving her the opportunity to eat more than one because it can cause a tummy upset. Note the exact time of the first birth, and of the presence of the placenta, because a retained placenta can cause infection later on.

The remaining puppies will make their appearance at intervals of anything from twenty minutes to an hour or so, between which the mother will rest and may take a drink of water or milk. An interval of move than two hours between births is a cause for concern and you should call the vet. During each birth it is a good idea to take the previous puppies and place them in the prepared box with the hot water bottle in it, returning them to their mother's nipples between times. When all the puppies have arrived, try the mother with a drink of warm milk and glucose, then take her out to relieve herself before she settles down for a well-earned rest with her new family.

Use the time while the bitch is out of the room to weigh the puppies for the first time. At birth Shih Tzu puppies weigh 4–8oz (113–226g). Not everyone bothers to weigh them regularly, but in my view there are two good reasons for doing so. The first is that, in the early weeks of life, the weight of a puppy is a good indicator of its well-being: a puppy that is gaining weight is prospering, a puppy that is standing still needs watching, and a puppy that is losing weight is in trouble and requires immediate attention. The second reason for weighing puppies is a long-term one: by recording the weights of consecutive litters up to the age of one year, I have been able to estimate fairly accurately what the adult weight of any puppy is likely to be from quite an early age. These comparisons have, of course, been between puppies that have been related in some way, so my weight comparisons would not be valid for puppies from other families and lines. My practice has always been to weigh each puppy at birth, then every other day for two weeks, then weekly up to three months and finally once each month up to six months.

When to Call the Vet

It would be lovely if every whelping was an uncomplicated and happy event, as described above, but of course things can go wrong and when they do it is vital to get professional help as soon as possible. For this reason, it is wise to put your vet on the alert as soon as whelping begins, in case an emergency arises later. In the following situations, I would advise seeking veterinary help as soon as possible.

1. The bitch has a dark green and/or bloody discharge before any puppies have been born. This sort of discharge is normal after the birth of a puppy, but not before.

2. The bitch has been having contractions and straining for two hours and nothing has happened. To wait longer may mean that she becomes exhausted and cannot deliver any of her puppies unaided.

3. You are sure there is one or more puppy yet to come, but the bitch has ceased straining for over two hours.

4. A puppy is present in the birth canal but appears to be stuck: in this case do not wait even ten minutes, as unless it is delivered quickly it will die, particularly if the bag of membranes has broken.

Complications in Whelping

Uterine Inertia

Two sorts of inertia can occur: primary inertia, when the bitch does not start contractions at all, and secondary inertia, when she becomes exhausted and contractions weaken or cease. Whatever the reason for inertia, veterinary help is required. This may take the form of an injection, or the vet may decide that the bitch needs a Caesarean section.

Caesarean Section

This will be undertaken only as a last resort, and is not a common occurrence in Shih Tzus, since puppies are normally delivered naturally despite their comparatively large heads. The breeder's problem after a Caesarean is that the bitch may not be willing to accept her puppies once she has recovered from the anaesthetic. You will have to encourage her to lick the puppies if possible, and to let them feed. Constant supervision will be required for the first few days, but by then she should hopefully have taken to her babies and will be able to rear them as usual. If she is not making milk as a result of the operation, the puppies will have to be hand-reared. This is hard work and very time-consuming, but it can be done with persistence and dedication (*see* below).

Breech Birth

Instead of arriving in the world head first, some puppies put in an appearance rump first. They are often born without trouble, but should a puppy's head become stuck, help must be given without delay. Grip the puppy with a clean piece of towel, being careful not to squeeze or crush the fragile body. At the bitch's next contraction, pull gently but firmly downwards as the bitch strains. Stop as soon as the contraction ceases, and wait for the next one before pulling again. It may help to turn the pup slightly from one side to the other as you pull.

Reviving Newborn Puppies

If a puppy is not breathing when it is born, first rub it vigorously with a dry, warm towel, and check that the mouth and nose are clear of fluid and mucus. If that does not work, take the pup in both hands (with fingers to each side of the neck so that it cannot slip from your grasp), and, holding it out in front of you with the head away from your body, swing it sharply downwards and bring it back up. Try placing a drop of brandy on the tongue, which will often cause the whelp to start breathing. Do not give up too soon: it is amazing how often an apparently lifeless puppy will suddenly gasp or choke and begin to take hold on life. As soon as you have succeeded in getting the breathing started, get the puppy dry and warm as soon as possible.

Inexperienced breeders are often afraid of handling the new whelps so firmly because they seem so fragile. However, if you watch a bitch who knows what she is about, you will see that she will be quite rough with her babies, pushing them about the bed and licking them so vigorously that they roll over and over.

Postnatal Care of the Bitch

During the first three weeks or so, if everything goes according to plan, the bitch will look after her puppies. It is your job to take care of all her needs. For the first forty-eight hours I would strongly recommend constant supervision. The new mother, especially if it is her first time in this role, may be so restless that she does not lie down long enough for the puppies to suckle: in this case it may be necessary to keep her still and put the puppies to the nipples, making sure that each puppy is sucking strongly. When they have fed, the mother will lick the puppies, not only to clean them but also to stimulate them to urinate and defecate – watch to see that the bitch is doing this, and watch out too that she does not lie on her babies when resting between feeds.

It is quite normal for the bitch to have a discharge after the births, dark in colour and blood-stained. It should diminish to nothing in a week or two, but in the meantime she will have to be kept clean.

When you bathe her rear end make sure she is fully dried before she goes back to the puppies. The bedding will also need to be changed on a regular basis, especially if the discharge is heavy at first. Her temperature may be up by a degree or so, but this should drop to normal by the fourth day.

At first the bitch may be disinclined to eat much, but encourage her to drink as much as possible. Persevere if she still refuses food after the first day, because she needs to keep up her strength in water to continue to make milk. As the days go by, the bitch needs more and more nourishment, so offer three or four meals a day or even more if she seems to want them. A high-protein diet is important for a nursing dam, and I always offer full-cream milk to drink as well as a plentiful supply of fresh water.

Examine the bitch's teats every day, to check for any signs of swelling. If one of the breasts becomes hard and swollen, and feels hot, it is probably because the milk is not being drawn off. It may be that the teat is not being used because there are only a few puppies, or because the nipple is inverted so that the pups cannot successfully fasten onto it. In either case some of the milk needs to be expressed, which will ease the condition. I recently learned of a simple way to draw off the unused milk, a method that works even with an inverted nipple, and only wish that I had known of it years ago. Cut the nozzle off a small syringe (the 2ml size), and then smooth the cut edge. Next smear the cut edge with a drop of olive oil, push in the plunger and place the syringe over the affected nipple. As the plunger is gently withdrawn, the milk will be removed with no discomfort to the bitch. This method is particularly useful if a teat is surplus to requirements, as in the case of a small litter, because it does not stimulate production of more milk to anything like the same degree as expressing the milk by manipulation. If a swollen teat is neglected, it can lead to an abscess developing or to mastitis.

Postnatal Care of the Puppies

Watching a litter of Shih Tzus grow is totally fascinating. The rate of growth and development is amazing: in the first week they are likely to double their birth weight. Puppies find their way to their mother to feed, and in between meals at the milk bar they tend to gather together and sleep in a heap. They rarely cry unless they are hungry or hurting in some way, and they look chubby and sturdy – a

Clover shows off her puppies just a few days after they are born.
(Photo: Yvonne Hyde.)

contented puppy, asleep on its back with a full tummy, bears a resemblance to a beached whale. At birth the Shih Tzu puppy does not look much like an adult: its nose, lips and eye rims are pink for the first few days, the eyes are shut for the first ten days or so, as are the ears, and even the colour of the short coat may be misleading. This is especially true of the gold shades; black and white pups are more likely to keep their colouring. The stump of the umbilical cord withers and falls off after a few days.

If the mother is coping well with her babies, feeding them and cleaning them satisfactorily, you should interfere as little as possible. Concentrate on providing the optimum environment for the new family, which includes warmth and freedom from drafts, and clean, dry bedding with a non-slip surface for when the babies start to walk. The best ambient temperature in the first week is 80–85°F (26.5–29.5°C). Any puppy that becomes chilled is in real peril, because its temperature will drop very rapidly and it will soon become too weak to move or even to suck if put to the teat. Should this happen, warm the puppy at once, but gradually. The best way to do this is by popping it next to your skin so that it can absorb your own body warmth. A hot-water bottle or heating pad is too extreme. Once the puppy is revived it can be put back to the mother to nurse,

167

For the first week or so, Clover's puppies spend all their time eating and sleeping. (Photo: Yvonne Hyde.)

but it cannot digest food whilst its temperature is low. The important thing is not to give up too easily: it has been known for a puppy suffering from hypothermia to be revived six or more hours after it collapsed.

Nails and Dew-Claws

Dogs are born with dew-claws, sometimes on the hind feet as well as the front. If you want the dew-claws removed, ask the vet to do it when the puppies are three or four days old. Removal of the dew-claws may be quite a good idea, since their presence can cause a lot of trouble in later life. I once came across an adult Shih Tzu whose dew-claws had been neglected and had grown right round and into the flesh, causing infection and evidently giving the poor little dog enormous pain. Do not have the mother present when the dew-claws are removed, as she will become extremely distressed should one of the puppies cry. I must own that I do not myself have the dew-claws removed because I am fearful of the effects of such a trauma on very young puppies, especially if they have been born two or more days prematurely.

From the time when they are two to three weeks old the puppies will need to have their sharp little nails regularly trimmed with scissors, or the mother will soon become sore and scratched as they pummel her tummy while they suckle. Depending on the floor surface upon which a Shih Tzu lives, this nail trimming will be a necessity throughout its adult life.

First Steps

Once the eyes are open, the puppies are more mobile and take more interest in their surroundings. At the age of about three weeks, they start to get up on their feet, usually coming up first on their front legs to raise their chests from the ground, and then lifting onto their rear legs to take those first wobbly steps. The exception to this is the flat puppy, one that lies with his legs sticking out at the corners and does not seem able to draw them underneath his body. Rearing puppies on a smooth surface can predispose them to this condition, which is why newspaper is so unsuitable for bedding. I have never had a flat puppy, or 'swimmer', but I am told that you should stand them several times a day, helping them to walk by supporting them with your hand, and by taping from elbow to elbow so that the legs are held under the body – I would seek a vet's advice before trying this though.

One of the magic moments, should you be lucky enough to observe it, is when a puppy first discovers that it is possible to move backwards as well as forwards. Another is the discovery of play, and from this time on the character of each individual puppy seems to develop apace. At this stage, from when they are about three or four weeks old, they need more space than the whelping bed can provide, so it is time to move them to a puppy pen. Ideally, one with one side of the

Clover's puppies at three week. (Photo: Yvonne Hyde.)

pen should be lower than the other three in order to enable the mother to hop in and out as she wishes, because she will not feel the need to be constantly with her babies as she has done hitherto.

I cannot stress enough how important it is that the flooring of the pen should not be smooth or shiny. However hygienic such surfaces may be, they are simply too slippery, and the progress of the puppies will be slowed down if their little feet are forever sliding from under them. My choice is a flannelette sheet, laid over several thicknesses of newspaper and anchored very firmly all round the edges outside the pen so that it cannot ruck up. On top of this, in one corner, stand a small low-sided bed which the pups can easily climb in and out of; they will instinctively choose to relieve themselves at the other side of the pen, away from this 'nest', and this in itself is a step towards house-training. Later on, say when they are six weeks old, the sheeting can be taken out and newspaper left in the corner the puppies are using as a toilet. They will tug at the newspaper and chew it and make a terrific mess, but constant clearing up is one of the regular chores to which all breeders have to resign themselves.

The puppy pen must be large enough to give plenty of room for running about by the time the puppies are six weeks old. Toys can be provided to stimulate play, such as a ball and soft toys. Common sense must be used, of course, and you must not give them anything

Puppies at the age of four weeks. (Photo: Jim Grugan.)

Puppies enjoy playing with a wide variety of toys.

that they can get into their mouths and swallow. Improvised toys are often as good as the most expensive bought ones, and I have found that an old golden syrup tin sealed up with pebbles inside it (for rolling around and for making a satisfying noise), or a sturdy cardboard box (for rushing in and out of, or just for demolishing) can provided endless fun. Some breeders have a special room set aside for whelping and puppy rearing, often a spare bedroom, but there are advantages if the puppy pen is set somewhere in the living area of the home. That way, the puppies become accustomed to the noises of domestic living, the hoover and the washing machine, and are also more exposed to human company. Little tails wag at the sound of a voice much sooner when the litter is being reared in this way. From the breeder's point of view, it is also nice to have the litter where they can be watched and picked up for a cuddle without making a special trip upstairs. One lady I knew always kept her litters in a pen under her huge kitchen table: they were always marvellously confident and outgoing puppies and absolutely nothing seemed to faze them.

Weaning

The process of weaning can be started in the fourth week, and by the time the whelps are eight weeks old they should be fully weaned and independent of their mother, although she will still like to spend time with them and play with them from time to time. It does not do to be

171

dogmatic about when to start, and much will depend on how well the bitch is coping and indeed how many puppies there are for her to keep up with. For the first few days, weaning is not so much a matter of getting large amounts of nourishment into the puppies to supplement their mother's milk as of getting the idea across, starting with lapping from a small bowl. I start weaning with a mixture of half unsweetened evaporated milk and half water, and after a week or so I change this to half evaporated and half cow's milk. Dipping a finger into the milk and then holding this to the puppies' noses will often get them started, but don't be surprised if they are not very interested, especially if they are getting plenty of milk from the dam.

Once the whelps have started to lap, it is time to introduce solid food, usually in the fourth week. Before the advent of all the special puppy foods that are now available, we always did very well with lean raw beef, scraped up off a lump of meat with a blunt knife into tiny balls. At first each puppy should be offered barely a teaspoon of such meat for each feed. By the time they are five or six weeks old the amount of meat can be increased to an ounce at each meal, and the meat can be finely minced rather than so laboriously scraped. Cooked chicken can also be added to the menu. Poached fish, cut very small, is a nutritious alternative to meat, but be very careful that there are no bones left in it. Eggs are always a useful addition to the diet so long as they are either hard-boiled or scrambled until cooked right through. Milk continues to be fed after the introduction of meat to the diet, until by the age of eight weeks the puppies are having two milky feeds and two of meat each day, perhaps still topped up by their mother overnight. Spend plenty of time supervising the puppies as they feed, and make sure that they are all getting a good share; except for the milk, I think it is worthwhile trying to feed them from separate bowls so that you can be sure all are eating well, but this is not exactly easy with a large litter of pups milling round and round!

The alternative to preparing food yourself is to use one of the ready-made products sold specifically for weaning puppies. There are tinned foods available, as well as dried ones, and all are manufactured to provide the necessary nutrients for a young puppy. If you use one of these it is important to follow the manufacturer's instructions carefully. However, if I was starting to wean a litter tomorrow, I would still use my tried and tested method of a variety of freshly prepared foods. This is not only because it has always worked so well for those of us who have done it for years, but also because I believe that when the puppies go to their new homes they will settle to a new regime much more easily if they have been eating a variety of foods previously. As a breeder, you cannot expect the new owner of your puppy to stick rigidly to exactly what you have been using. Indeed, many pet owners will use tinned food sooner rather than later on account of its convenience and ready availability in the supermarkets.

Occasionally the introduction of solid food can cause loose stools, in which case a good remedy is to crumble into the meat one of the small rice cakes that are sold in the baby departments of high street chemists and supermarkets. Another useful baby food is rusks, which can be soaked into the milk feeds at first and then provided whole to be chewed on after the arrival of the first teeth. At eight weeks of age, Shih Tzu puppies should be having four or five meals each day, high in protein and with variety of content; as long as you get them off to a good start, healthy eating is largely a matter of habit, and the competition between litter-mates is a good stimulus to this. Clean water must be available at all times from now on, even if they paddle in it and make a mess!

Worming

Puppies should be wormed at three weeks of age, and again at five, eight and twelve weeks. The best product to use is one recommended by the vet rather than something picked up at the local pet shop, and you must follow the instructions exactly. The fact that a bitch has been wormed prior to whelping does not protect the puppies from having worms. Should a puppy have worms it will appear to be pot-bellied and dull of coat, and if untreated will certainly not thrive.

Teething

A puppy is born with no teeth at all, and starts to acquire his first set at about three or four weeks of age. There should be twenty-eight teeth in all (fourteen less than should appear in the second and final set), with six incisors, top and bottom, at the front. I mention the incisors particularly because these are sometimes a problem for the prospective show puppy if one or more is missing. The presence of a full complement of incisors in the first set of teeth does not guarantee that there will the same when the permanent teeth come in. On the other hand, missing incisors at the baby teeth stage bodes ill for the next set. The presence and placement of the incisors is important in the show ring, but makes not a jot of difference to the functionality of the teeth – since, with a level or slightly undershot jaw, the Shih Tzu's incisors may be regarded as more cosmetic than anything else. These first teeth are like little needles, and their arrival is enough to make most bitches lose some interest in the process of nursing their babies.

Postnatal Complications

So far, I have described the postnatal care and development of a healthy litter of puppies, but there are a few problems that may crop up, and it is as well to be forewarned of what just might go wrong. The novice breeder who has a little knowledge of what sort of problems may occur is all the better equipped to cope with complications.

Hand-Rearing Puppies

You may have to deal with puppies which are orphaned or which must be hand-reared because the bitch is unable to feed and care for them for some reason. It would be dishonest of me to pretend that hand-rearing puppies is easy; it is in truth both exhausting and stressful, with no guarantee of success. It can be done, but it is really a job for more than one person unless you can manage without sleep for days on end. Feeding must be carried out every two or three hours, day and night, for the first two weeks. Thereafter, the number of feeds can be gradually reduced as the amount taken per meal increases.

First you must decide what to use as a milk formula. Everyone seems to have their own ideas about this, and you can use commercially prepared brands of milk substitute or home-made recipes. My own favourite is half and half evaporated milk and boiled water, which I use unsweetened, although others tell me they add a drop of glucose or honey. Goat's milk is regarded as better than cow's, as it is higher in fat and thus more like that of the bitch. Whatever milk is used, warm it to blood temperature but no more, and be extra careful if a microwave is used for heating as it may cause hot spots in the liquid.

There are three ways of getting nourishment into the pup: by bottle, by dropper or by tube. The last involves inserting a tube into the stomach, and should never be attempted without expert help, since the result will be fatal if the wrong length of tube is used or if the tube enters the lung instead of the stomach. Similarly, dropper-feeding carries with it the risk of milk entering the lung, but it may be the only way to feed a puppy which is too weak to suck, or if you lack the expertise to use a tube. When feeding by dropper, lay the pup on its front or side in your lap and place one drop at a time on the front of the tongue. This is very time-consuming, but it simply cannot be hurried because each drop must be swallowed before the next is popped into place. Bottle-feeding is somewhat easier, so long as the bottle is of a suitable size (bottles sold for cat-feeding are fairly easy to find at pet shops) and if the teat has the right size of hole. Too small a hole will mean that the pup will not be able to get enough, too large may cause choking; if the hole is the right size, the milk will just drip slowly from it when the bottle is inverted. Again, settle the pup into your lap, and make sure that when the teat goes into its mouth the tongue is underneath.

All of this is a real labour of love, and the breeder who carries out these tasks every other hour will become very bonded with the puppies in his or her care. After every meal, the processes of urination and defecation need to be stimulated by mimicking the action of the mother's tongue over the stomach and genital region using a moist piece of cotton wool. With a large litter, by the time the last puppy has been fed, emptied and cleaned, and the equipment all cleaned and sterilized, it is nearly time to start preparing the next round of feeds. As someone once said to me, it makes you sympathize with Old Mother Hubbard.

Fading Puppy Syndrome

This term is used to describe one of the most devastating situations with which any breeder can be faced. Seemingly healthy puppies begin quite literally to fade away, losing weight, losing the desire to feed and dehydrating fast, often crying ceaselessly with a heartbreakingly high-pitched whine, apparently losing the will to live until one by one they die. No single disease has been identified as the cause of the condition, although several environmental factors are believed to contribute.

Of the three sorts of micro-organism that are believed to play a part, the bacterial infections are perhaps best known, especially Beta haemolytic streptococcus and E-coli. It has been suggested that Beta haemolytic streptococcus infection is more likely to cause individual puppies to fade, whereas E-coli may be responsible for the fading of whole litters. Individual resistance to these infections will vary, depending on the stage of pregnancy at which the infection was contracted, the severity of the infection, the strength of the puppy, and so on. Fading in puppies may be caused by toxoplasmosis rather than bacterial infection, and a third cause may be the canine virus hepatitis. Only a post-mortem will diagnose the cause of death in any one case with certainty. Infections may arise through the umbilicus, or through ingestion after birth, or by environmental contamination. Parasites are common carriers of infection. An additional complication can be dehydration, which may arise as a symptom of any of these infections. This can be tested for by pinching up a fold of a puppy's skin between thumb and forefinger: if the skin remains folded up or is very slow to go back, then this is an indication of dehydration.

Hypothermia may cause fading in puppies. As I have already mentioned, for the first week a puppy requires an ambient temperature of over 80°F (26.5°C) and from the second to fourth weeks of life it should be in the high 70s°F (around 25°C). Few breeders attempt to maintain these high temperatures in one whole room in the house, hence the use of supplementary heating devices. It is not a good idea to suspend an infra-red lamp over the whelping bed of the Shih Tzu, because it is likely to make the heavily coated mother uncomfortable. There is also a danger that such a lamp may set up convection currents that draw a draught up over the puppies' backs, and result in other problems.

It is said that as many as a quarter of all live-born puppies die before they are weaned. Some die because of congenital abnormalities, such as cleft palate, and others from accidents or bad mothering, but a larger proportion than is generally accepted may fall victim to one or more of the factors that are said to play a part in fading puppy syndrome. Treatment may be efficacious in some cases, but a better answer is to set up a first line of defence as follows:

1. Vaccinate all dogs on the premises and keep up the boosters regularly.

2. Discuss with your veterinary adviser the possibility of using antibiotics strategically, on the bitch at the time of mating, during pregnancy and at whelping. Certainly this might be a wise course in a situation where a previous litter of puppies has died.

3. Carry out a regular and conscientious worming regime for all your dogs, with extra worming treatment for the pregnant bitch and the appropriate doses for the puppies as they grow.

4. Disinfect premises where dogs are kept, especially the area used as whelping accommodation, and insist on strict hygiene in dog food preparation areas.

5. Burn all dog excreta, or otherwise dispose of it as soon as possible.

6. Prevent the risk of hypothermia by exercising strict temperature control during the first weeks of the puppy's life.

All of this can be summed up as the adoption of sound husbandry practices, or more simply as just good common sense whether or not puppies are being reared on the premises. If a sensible regime is adhered to in this way, the possibility of complications arising is much reduced, and the result will hopefully be a healthy litter of puppies for the bitch and her breeder to enjoy to the full.

Mastitis

Mastitis occurs if one of the breasts becomes infected. It causes the mother to run a high temperature and to become listless and refuse her food as the pain increases. It is a condition that requires immediate veterinary treatment, usually including antibiotics. Puppies must not be permitted to suck from an infected teat as they risk being infected by the milk, so the teat must be taped or bound up (although this must be done under the guidance of the vet, who will instruct you on the day-to-day care of the bitch with mastitis).

Eclampsia

Eclampsia is one of the most serious conditions that can affect the nursing bitch, and is caused by a low level of calcium. It can occur early after whelping or at any time while the bitch is nursing her puppies, and is marked by restlessness, lethargy and a high temperature, with panting and hysteria. The affected bitch sometimes walks around with a stiff-legged gait, and if help is not immediately obtained she may have fits and collapse. This is one of those times when veterinary attention must be sought without delay, as the condition is life-threatening. Although most bitches respond very well to treatment (intravenous injections of calcium) it usually means that the puppies will have to be taken off the dam and fed by the breeder, for a time at least.

Naming Puppies

Shih Tzus go through life equipped with two names. One is the official name, by which the dog is registered at the Kennel Club and entered at shows: this name may include the 'family' name or affix, which the breeder has registered for his or her exclusive use, and must consist of more than one word but not more than twenty-four letters. As a breed archivist, how I have called down curses on the heads of breeders who have chosen elaborate and obscure names for their Shih Tzus! Over the years these become misspelt until they are almost unrecognizable. Please, please choose a name that errs on the side of simplicity and which is easy to spell and to pronounce, remembering that this is to your advantage as well. Because of the character and illustrious antecedents of the Shih Tzu, I should be sad to see one named in a facetious or scatological manner, but happily this has so far never happened in Britain and I trust the Kennel Club would never allow it.

The other name is the pet name, the one by which the dog will be known at home, and it is rarely the same as the official registered name. Indeed, many of the latter would be quite impractical for daily use. Sometimes the breeder will have given the puppies pet names and sometimes not: in my own case I try to avoid it since it can make it even harder to part with them, and in any case the new owners will probably have their own ideas. Whether you are a breeder or buyer, it is worth bearing in mind that the name should be easily distinguishable from that of any other dog in the household, and that it should trip off the tongue readily in most circumstances. I once fancied calling a pretty little bitch by what I considered to be a lovely name (I must decline to tell you what it was), but my husband absolutely refused to go into the garden and call it out!

11

Ailments and Diseases

The Shih Tzu is generally a healthy breed, plagued by few serious hereditary diseases. If well bred and carefully reared, these are sturdy and robust little dogs, so with luck the majority of owners may never come across most of the problems to which I refer in this chapter. However, when illness does strike, early detection and treatment is the key to a happy outcome. Owners need to be able to recognize the symptoms that indicate ailments and diseases. I do not include treatment here except for the most minor of conditions, because diagnosis and treatment are the province of the vet.

First-Aid Kit

My list of essential first-aid items for dogs includes things you would expect to find in a first-aid kit for humans, plus a few extras that I have found useful in the care of my Shih Tzus:

Cotton wool   For swabbing minor wounds, cleaning eyes and other uses.
Bandages
Thermometer, blunt-ended   A digital thermometer is easiest to read.
Antiseptic powder   For dressing cuts and scratches.
Artificial tears   For cleaning and lubricating eyes.
Paediatric kaolin   For diarrhoea.
Milk of magnesia   For mild gastritis or liverishness.
Aspirin   For the relief of pain from such conditions as arthritis or muscle strains, but to be used only under veterinary supervision.
Permanganate of potash or styptic pencil   To prevent bleeding from a badly cut nail.

Many of these items are kept in my ever-present grooming box, and all of them are always at hand. They have carried me safely through all the minor crises of life with my Shih Tzus. For anything more serious, I have always taken the dog to see the vet. Finding a good vet is a priority for any dog owner and the relationship between you should ideally be a partnership, in which you play your part by observing and keeping careful notes of any symptoms. This will greatly help the vet in his diagnosis.

Nursing a Sick Shih Tzu

Care of a sick dog involves taking careful notes of all symptoms and progress, and by notes I really do mean writing everything down, because it is so easy to forget something when you are anxious. If your vet has given you medicine, it is vital to administer this to the patient at exactly the times and in the precise doses prescribed. Generally speaking, a sick dog should be kept somewhere quiet and well away from other dogs and children, and not only when an infectious disease is involved. Most sick dogs will probably prefer to be left in peace, but there are occasions when the patient becomes anxious without the reassurance of close contact with its owner, so peace and quiet does not mean total isolation.

If a dog has to undergo surgery, the vet will usually advise you that no food or drink must be given the night before the operation. It is important to obey these instructions, as otherwise there is a danger that a dog will vomit while he is anaesthetized. If your dog does manage to get hold of something to eat during the period when food should not have been taken, confess this to the vet and leave it to him to decide whether or not it is necessary to postpone the operation.

Once your pet has had surgery and is safely back home, the first twenty-four hours or so are the most critical. If you have become adept at taking the temperature, and can do this without disturbing or distressing the patient, you will be able to watch out for any sudden rise or fall, and can report it to the vet. As well as keeping the dog quiet and warm, and providing fresh water and food according to the vet's instructions, keep an eye open for such things as a failure to urinate or defecate over a period and for traces of blood in either waste product. Watch that the dog does not try to chew at stitches or remove a bandage if there is one in place.

Most of us are reluctant to bother our vets unnecessarily, but if you are worried about anything at all during the period of recovery after an operation, it is better to get in touch straight away than to leave things as they are.

Taking the Temperature

The dog's temperature should be taken rectally, by inserting the thermometer up to an inch but no more, and leaving it for a minute (or however long the instructions with the thermometer require) before carefully withdrawing it. Use petroleum jelly to grease the end of the thermometer before you begin, and if possible have a helper to raise the dog's tail firmly and hold it up so that he cannot sit down. This procedure is simpler to carry out than to describe, and I have never met a dog that minded in the least. The normal canine temperature is 101.4°F (39°C). Any significant deviation from this may be an indication that something is wrong, particularly if combined with other symptoms, so it is useful to be able to take your dog's temperature and is something every owner should become familiar with. Take your dog's temperature once or twice when you don't actually need to: practising in this way will make it much less stressful to take the temperature when you are really worried about a sick dog.

Administering Medicines Orally

To get a pill into a dog, place your thumb and middle finger behind the top canine teeth and open the mouth by lifting the upper jaw. Place the pill at the back of the throat with the other hand, being sure to put it in the centre of the back of the tongue and not to one side. Then close the dog's mouth and hold it closed while stroking the throat until he swallows the pill. That is the theory, but getting a pill into a Shih Tzu is not always this easy, or so I have found. I have watched other owners do it many times, but when it is my turn the dogs tend to spit out the pill as soon as I release my hold on their muzzles. My favourite alternative strategy is to hide the pill in a favourite titbit. Should even that fail, the pill can be broken up and placed in a spot of honey on the dog's tongue – this is much harder to spit out and usually goes down.

Giving liquid medicines orally is much easier. Just lift the upper lip at the side, and pour the medicine into the mouth from a spoon or a dropper, holding the mouth shut until the liquid is swallowed. If your dog resists, ask the vet for a syringe without a needle, and place the liquid medicine in this. I have also used a syringe in this way to give a drink of water to a very sick dog on occasions, and found it easy to dribble a little liquid at a time onto the tongue.

Accidents and Emergencies

When an accident occurs, whether it is a road traffic incident, a car crash or a minor injury in the home, the dog may be more hurt than is immediately apparent. He may have internal injuries, and there is also a possibility that he will go into a state of shock. Both conditions need professional veterinary attention, and this should be obtained without delay. Meanwhile, move the dog as little as possible, and keep him warm by covering him lightly with a blanket or coat.

Anyone who goes to the assistance of a dog that has been involved in an accident should proceed with extreme caution. We all want to help in such a situation, but any animal, whether or not it knows us, may be likely to bite if it is frightened, hurt, in pain or in a state of shock. Take sensible precautions when handling any injured animal.

Burns

Every home holds dangers for the domestic pet, especially for a lively puppy which is always either underfoot or poking its nose into everything. Fortunately, the heavy Shih Tzu coat provides a good degree of protection from such minor mishaps as splashes of hot water or fat, or from sunburn in normal conditions. Apply a cold compress to relieve the pain and in any serious case involving burns or scalding do seek veterinary help immediately.

Heatstroke

Apply cold water or an ice pack, or resort to the more drastic remedy of immersing the dog completely in cold water to alleviate the effects of heatstroke. It may be caused by leaving a dog in a car in hot weather for even the shortest of times, or even by being in the sun on a very hot summer's day. A Shih Tzu suffering from heat stroke will be in evident distress, panting frantically and sometimes dribbling thick saliva, and showing increased redness of the lips and tongue. Any dog in such a condition needs to be treated at once to reduce the temperature because there is nothing it can do to help itself. Prevention is better than cure: no dog should ever be left unattended in a car (even if the sun does not seem to be so very hot, the temperature inside the vehicle will rise very quickly), nor should it be confined in hot unventilated quarters or over-exercised during the heat of the day.

Poisoning

However careful you are, there is always the possibility of a dog, and especially a puppy, picking up and eating something it shouldn't, so constant vigilance is required to prevent this happening. Most people know that some of the things used in the garden, such as slug pellets, are poisonous to animals and so are careful never to use these when they own dogs. Another source of danger is poisonous plants, such as laburnum and some bulbs and fungi. Poisonous products in the house include disinfectants, some detergents, paint and paint remover, none of which would be particularly palatable to an adult dog but any of which might be taken by a curious puppy: keep them out of reach. Medication for both dogs and people must be stored in a place which is as inaccessible to dogs as it is to small children.

Some of the symptoms of poisoning include violent and sudden sickness, an unsteady gait or collapse, and loss of consciousness. Anyone who has reason to suspect that their dog has taken poison should get to a vet immediately without even stopping to think about it. To delay is to risk losing the dog. If possible, take along some of the substance the dog has ingested, so that your vet knows precisely what he is dealing with. It is worth mentioning that if you know your dog has swallowed a corrosive substance (such as bleach or anti-freeze), you must in no circumstances attempt to make the dog vomit.

Pyometra

A disease exclusive to bitches, and more common in those over six years of age, pyometra occurs in the period up to twelve weeks following the end of a bitch's season, and is a danger to life if not dealt with at once. The bitch with pyometra becomes depressed and lethargic, refusing to take food yet inclined to drink more than usual, while at the same time the tummy may become distended, all of this happening within a short time. If the condition is what is known as an 'open' pyometra there will be a discharge of pus from the uterus, but with the 'closed' type there is no such symptom because the pus accumulates within the uterus. The usual outcome of this disease is that a hysterectomy has to be performed, the sooner the better.

Stings

As Shih Tzus have such curious and enquiring natures they are quite liable to get stung, particularly puppies. A bee or a wasp can cause a painful swelling. In the case of a bee sting, remove the sting before applying a solution of bicarbonate of soda. Other insects do not leave their stings in their victims. For wasp stings the best treatment is to apply a little vinegar to the wound.

General Health Problems

Anal Glands

These two small glands are located just inside the anus and contain a fluid that is extremely malodorous and which is normally expressed by the pressure of defecation. Sometimes the glands become too full, the discomfort of which may cause the dog to drag his rear across the ground, and when this occurs it may be advisable to remove the excess fluid by squeezing the glands. A vet will do this, and will also show the owner how to do it if necessary, as when the anal sacs are failing to empty naturally for one reason or another. Only one of my Shih Tzus has ever had this problem, and it was caused, so my vet told me, by the anal glands being too deeply seated for the normal pressure of defecation to clear them out. We learned to recognize the signs, such as when the dog scooted along on his bottom or turned sharply and repeatedly to bite at his rear, and were taught to deal with the situation ourselves.

Back Problems

I do not know how widespread these problems are in the breed. Sometimes one hears nothing about back problems for a year or more, but when I once mentioned a Shih Tzu with a back problem in my weekly breed notes for the canine press, the response was a whole spate of letters about just this sort of case. Most back problems seem to be the result of injury or strain, or are of what I would call the 'slipped disc' variety, although that may be a misnomer.

Symptoms include pain, difficulty in walking, unsteadiness on the back legs, and in some cases complete paralysis of the rear quarters, together with the inability to control urination. The cases about which I have been told have tended to involve older Shih Tzus rather than very young ones. Sometimes the owner was aware of an incident that caused the back problem, such as the dog leaping from the furniture and landing badly, but on other occasions the problem seemed to arise suddenly and for no apparent reason. The vet may recommend complete rest with medication, and this can be sufficient to effect an improvement, but sometimes an operation may be required.

Halitosis (Bad Breath)

The most common cause of bad breath is tooth decay, although it may also be caused by gum infection or by the wrong diet. You can buy toothpaste for dogs, and brushing the teeth once or twice a week with this will really help to keep them clean and free from tartar. Brushing the teeth daily will be even better. Giving the dog hard dog biscuits or nylon bones to chew will also clean the teeth, whereas a diet consisting exclusively of soft, tinned food will tend to encourage the formation of tartar. If your Shih Tzu has smelly breath, and tends to rub his face along the floor or furniture, these are warning signs that tooth decay may be present. Bad teeth must be dealt with immediately, because unless they are extracted their presence is likely to lead to gum disease as well as inhibiting the dog from eating properly. Regular inspection of the teeth and gums will prevent matters from ever reaching that stage.

Sometimes halitosis can occur as a result of a stomach disorder or kidney disease, so persistent bad breath is not a symptom which should ever be disregarded.

Constipation

A symptom of constipation most owners will easily be able to recognize is that the dog strains to defecate but is unable to do so, or will cry out with the effort to relieve himself. One of the first things to check is that there is not a stool caught in the hair around the anus, thereby causing a physical blockage. Shih Tzus will defecate once or twice each day on average, and as it is the owner's job to clear up the faeces daily it is easy to take note of any problems in this respect.

A small dose of liquid paraffin can be given as a mild laxative so long as the constipation is not habitual, or alternatively the same quantity of olive oil added to the food may do the trick.

Rather than resort to laxatives, if your dog repeatedly suffers from constipation it is best to try to determine the cause, consulting with your vet if you need to. The wrong sort of diet has been known to be a contributory factor, for instance when the food lacks fibre, so changing a dog's food is often enough to solve the problem. Occasionally, an enlarged prostate gland in a male may cause straining and an inability to defecate, a condition that can only be diagnosed by rectal examination by a vet.

Coprophagy

Coprophagy is the eating of excreta, whether it is the dog's own or that of another animal. I do not know of any effective cure once the habit is ingrained; nor have I found any definitive explanation of why dogs do it, although it has been suggested that it is a dog's instinctive attempt to make up for a dietry deficiency. It often starts early in life, when a puppy will chew stones, earth, almost anything, especially when he is teething. Because it can so easily become a habit, it makes sense to pick up regularly after your dogs (which is in any case part of good basic husbandry) and so prevent their indulgence in this unpleasant behavior.

Cystitis

Cystitis is a bladder infection that causes a dog to urinate frequently, or to suffer pain when doing so. If he is unable to urinate this is more likely to be as a result of an obstruction in the bladder, probably stones (*see* Stones in the Bladder on page 192). Both conditions must be treated urgently.

Diarrhoea

Diarrhoea may simply be the result of overeating or of eating something unsuitable, but it may also be a symptom of a more serious disease. Only when I am quite sure that the diarrhoea is of the first sort do I attempt to treat it – otherwise I always take the dog to the vet. For a puppy or a very old dog diarrhoea is always potentially dangerous, since both can dehydrate very quickly indeed.

Treatment for a simple case of overeating is to fast the dog for a day and to give a small dose of paediatric kaolin. Only a light meal must be offered on the next day, even if the patient appears to be fully recovered – perhaps a little cooked chicken with plain boiled rice. However, it is extremely important never to withhold water, for a dog with diarrhoea must be allowed drink in order to combat dehydration. If my devotion to the Shih Tzu has ever wavered, it was when three of my little darlings all inflicted themselves with a bad case of 'the runs', with the result that I had to wash their trousers over and over again through the course of what seemed a never-ending day. To be fair, I should add that I bear a large part of the blame for this incident, because I had allowed them to gorge themselves with pieces of leftover Christmas turkey.

Distemper and Infectious Hepatitis

Fortunately, the existence of vaccines to protect against these extremely contagious diseases means that most of today's dog owners have never encountered them. Both used to be major problems for the canine population, and caused many deaths. So long as you have regular booster injections for your Shih Tzu each year, you should never have anything to worry about. Many vets send reminders to their clients when it is time for the next vaccination.

Ear Problems

When grooming around a Shih Tzu's ears, check beneath the flap. Persistent dirt can be a symptom of many different conditions, including canker, so seek veterinary advice without delay. Grass seeds (see page 188) can cause painful ear irritation, and sedation or even anaesthesia may be required in order to remove them. Other symptoms of ear trouble are when a dog holds his head to one side, rubs his ear on the floor or furniture, scratches at one ear incessantly or shakes his head repeatedly. An unpleasant smell from the ear also indicates the presence of infection.

Eye Problems

Eye problems are not unusual for the Shih Tzu because it has large, round, forward-facing eyes, which are particularly liable to be damaged. The eyes must be kept very clean, and it is best to wash round them daily to prevent any build-up of discharge. At the same time, check the surface of the eyeball for damage.

When the surface of the eye becomes dry through lack of tears, the dog is said to have dry eye syndrome. I have found it to be more common in older dogs than young ones. Artificial tears can relieve the dog's discomfort, but they do have to be used very regularly. It used to be necessary to consider an operation for persistent dry eye syndrome, but the vet now has the option to prescribe an ointment which will stimulate the tear glands to produce tears once more.

Ulceration of the eye will cause the Shih Tzu a lot of pain. Often it is only when he paws at his face and rubs his eye against furniture that an owner becomes aware of the problem. Fortunately eye ulcers heal well if detected early and if treated with a special ointment that your vet will prescribe. Two outbreaks of eye ulcers have cropped up recently in my house. One was caused by a young and playful puppy that scratched the eyes of some of my adult dogs as she waved her paws in their faces in play. The other situation arose when an elderly dog, beginning to lose some of the sharpness of his vision, suffered a series of ulcers from diving in and out of his favourite bush, catching his eye as he did so. The bush was cut back and the problem has not so far recurred.

Grass Seeds

Grass seeds are more than just a nuisance when they get into a Shih Tzu's coat. There is a danger that a seed will actually penetrate the skin, perhaps by lodging between the pads of the feet, or by getting up the nose or into the ear. Once under the skin the wretched thing can migrate from one site to another, and may cause an abscess if left undetected. To avoid this problem we are always careful to cut any grass before it goes to seed, and do not take the dogs for walks in long grass when it is seeding. Especially in the summer, be alert to the potential hazards of grass seeds.

Hernias

An umbilical hernia can readily be identified as a bulge on the dog's tummy around the area of the navel. An inguinal hernia will be found as a bulge in the groin region. Both are caused by the protrusion of part of an organ through the abdominal wall, and the seriousness of either will depend on its size. Sometimes a small hernia on a young puppy does not grow as the puppy does, so that by about six months of age the hernia has virtually disappeared. On the other hand, large hernias may need to be repaired, but this is not a serious operation. If you are purchasing a puppy as a pet, the presence of a hernia should not cause concern, although perhaps the price should be reduced to reflect the fact that surgery may be necessary after the age of about six months. A hernia can be a problem for a show dog, since the Kennel Club has in recent years considered the repair of a hernia as an act that alters the natural conformation of a dog, and consequently one which is prohibited by their regulations for the preparation of dogs for exhibition. I do regret this attitude on the part of the Kennel Club, because it may deter some thoughtless owners from having hernias repaired when they really should be. The repair of a hernia should be carried out on veterinary advice and for the good of the dog, without regard for show prospects. Because the incidence of hernias is today considered to be hereditary, it is recommended that bitches with hernias should not normally be bred from, nor should males with this condition be used at stud.

Kennel Cough

Kennel cough, a dry rough cough, has nothing to do with kennels except that it often used to be contracted when dogs were placed in boarding kennels, which is how it got its name. The infection is extremely contagious, so it would spread very quickly through a kennel establishment. Except in the case of young puppies, it is not usually a serious problem. The important thing is to isolate the affected Shih Tzu so that other dogs are not infected. No one should be so irresponsible as to take a dog with kennel cough into the company of others, let alone to a show. Affected dogs should be treated by a vet, but do not allow them to mix with other dogs in the vet's waiting room. There is a vaccination that can be given to provide protection against kennel cough.

Kidney Trouble

Shih Tzu owners in America and parts of Scandinavia seem to have been more concerned with kidney trouble than those in Britain, which is not to say that the condition is totally unknown here. Symptoms of kidney disease may include increased thirst, loss of weight and/or appetite, more frequent urination, a depressed attitude and a general lassitude. None of these should be ignored, and immediate veterinary advice must be sought, as there are several different kidney diseases and only an expert diagnosis will determine exactly what the problem is. Kidney problems are more likely to occur in older dogs.

Lameness

The most common cause of lameness in Shih Tzus is matting of the hair between the pads of the foot, sometimes with the added complication of grit or dried mud being impacted in the hair. Over-long nails can also cause lameness. With careful and regular checking of the feet as part of the routine grooming procedure, these problems should never arise. A minor strain or sprain, whether of muscles or tendons, will cause lameness, and I have found that very active dogs will occasionally suffer in this way from simply jumping and landing badly. When the dog shows no other signs of pain, a period of rest will usually be all that is needed to effect a quick cure in these cases.

There are, of course, other and more serious causes of lameness. These are more likely to cause a limp that continues and becomes progressively worse, and include hip dysplasia (responsible for lameness in the rear quarters), patella luxation and slipping hock (both of which occur when the ball of the joint slips out of its socket). In older dogs arthritis must also always be considered as a possible factor. Hip dysplasia normally affects larger breeds of dogs, and I have heard of only a handful of Shih Tzu cases in the last twenty-five years. If a bone has fractured or a joint become dislocated there is likely to be a sudden onset of severe pain, and the dog will be unable to put any weight on the affected limb. In these cases veterinary attention must be sought urgently.

Parasites

Parasites, whether internal or external, should never be tolerated because they are likely to affect the health and comfort of both dog and owner. Of the internal parasites, the roundworm, *Toxocara canis*, is the most common, and it is the one that has received the most publicity because in children blindness may result from an infection. The danger of the latter has been greatly exaggerated in the popular press, and if all dog owners regularly wormed their pets there would be no danger at all. Puppies should be wormed at three, five, eight and twelve weeks of age and then monthly until six months. Further worming treatment is advisable every three to six months or so, to guard against reinfestation.

The arrival of external parasites, such as fleas, lice, ticks and harvest mites, depends to some extent on where you live. When we lived in the depths of the countryside and had sheep as our neighbours, our dogs seemed to pick up ticks most summers, whereas since we moved to a suburban location we haven't seen one. Fleas are to my mind the most unwelcome visitors of all, since they breed so prolifically and are very hard to find in the profuse Shih Tzu coat. An added complication is that the eggs of the flea are laid in the dog's environment – in his bedding, and in soft furnishings and cracks in floorboards. The eggs hatch into larvae which will go into the pupal stage before emerging as adult fleas to start the whole process of infestation all over again.

Scratching is the most obvious symptom of flea infestation, although dogs vary in their sensitivity to flea bites. Sometimes it is possible to see flea faeces as tiny specks in the dog's coat, but it is hard to spot these amongst dark-coloured hairs. Fortunately, the dog owner's armoury against the flea is both varied and effective. Sprays, powders, shampoos and dips abound, of which my own preferred weapon is a good insecticidal shampoo or spray. It is essential to treat carpets, chairs and dog bedding at the same time and to repeat the treatment at regular intervals for several months if the premises become heavily infested. Flea collars can also be purchased to protect a dog against reinfestation, although I have not found them as effective as a good-quality spray. A new and very effective preparation is applied to the back of the dog's neck and so is easier to use with a heavily coated dog than sprays or powders. It is available on prescription only, from your vet.

Parvovirus

Few people had heard of parvovirus before the early 1970s, and it was frightening for dog owners to be faced with such an infectious and virulent disease. It is not normally a problem today because there are effective vaccines, kept up to date with annual boosters. Difficulties can arise, however, if the disease is contracted by young puppies at a time when they have lost the immunity received from the mother but are still too young to be vaccinated. One of the main symptoms is vomiting and severe diarrhoea, often with blood, and the puppy will soon become so dehydrated that it is impossible to administer enough fluid to save it. In such a case the best chance of saving the puppy is to have the vet put it on a drip. Someone who was unlucky enough to have a whole litter of puppies succumb to parvovirus told me that because all the adult dogs in the house were fully vaccinated there was no way to detect it until the puppies became ill. Cleaning and disinfecting his home proved extremely difficult because the virus is resistant to many domestic disinfectants.

Scratching

This symptom can indicate conditions I have mentioned elsewhere, such as fleas (*see* Parasites) or skin problems (*see* overleaf). Another possible cause of itchiness is some sort of allergy, perhaps to a food, or to one of the chemicals used in domestic cleaning agents, or indeed to almost anything else. Allergies are notoriously difficult to sort out, but if your dog is constantly scratching and you have eliminated the obvious causes mentioned above, you might experiment by changing the type of detergents used to wash dog bedding and the floors. Next, try changing the dog's shampoo and/or coat dressing to see if this helps. If this does not effect an improvement, a complete change of diet can be tried. Because of the long coat, a Shih Tzu that is continually scratching gets into a mess very quickly indeed, so this problem has to be sorted out both for the dog's comfort and for the purposes of showing. Otherwise the coat is soon lost and can take up to a year to grow again to show standard.

Skin Problems

Skin problems may be caused by mange, eczema (wet or dry), ringworm, seborrhea and many other conditions. Even vets sometimes find it difficult to determine what is causing a particular problem, and the attention of a skin specialist is often required. Some skin conditions, such as sarcoptic mange and ringworm, are infectious to humans as well as to other dogs, so scrupulous standards of hygiene must be maintained when you are looking after a dog with any of these. On the other hand, a dog with eczema will not infect others (it can be a clue to the condition if one dog is affected but not the others). On an optimistic note, I should say that in all the years I have owned Shih Tzus I have never come across any of these conditions. Seek advice and treatment as soon as possible, meanwhile isolating the affected dog both from other dogs and from children.

Stones in the Bladder

This is a condition that I have of heard in several Shih Tzus, and I had a distressing case in one of my own dogs many years ago. The first sign I noticed was that the dog was evidently having difficulty in passing urine, standing with his leg raised for ages but producing only a trickle. He was obviously in extreme discomfort and we had to use a catheter to relieve him. Our vet diagnosed the presence of stones and operated to remove them.

Bladder stones in the canine species are mostly associated with alkaline urine, so a change in diet may help to prevent their recurrence in an individual dog where analysis has shown that the urine is alkaline. Special diets are available for a dog suffering from stones, and may have to be used for the rest of the dog's life. It also seems that some lines are genetically more predisposed to forming stones than others, and that the Shih Tzu may be one of the breeds more vulnerable to this condition.

Teeth

(*See also* Bad Breath on page 185.)

The Shih Tzu teeth, particularly the incisors, have shallow roots compared with those of many other breeds of dog, so they tend to lose them sooner rather than later. It is by no means uncommon to meet a really elderly Shih Tzu with no teeth at all. They cope amazingly well without their teeth, even to the extent of disposing of quite hard food. We had one toothless old lady who always insisted on taking to bed a hard biscuit, just as she had throughout her life, and each morning it was gone completely, sucked and 'gummed' until she could swallow it.

Tight Nostrils

Even puppies born with wide nostrils can suffer from tight nostrils when getting their first and second teeth. The result of tight nostrils is that the puppy is unable to breathe easily through its nose. He will snuffle and wheeze, and may go off his food because breathing through the mouth makes sucking difficult. Once the teeth are through, the nostrils open up again. If an adult Shih Tzu has tight nostrils this is a different matter altogether. It is believed to be an inherited condition, seemingly rarer than it used to be in the breed ten years ago. Such a dog will snort and snuffle audibly after exercise or in hot weather, and should not be bred from.

Tumours

Finding a hard swelling or lump anywhere on a dog is an alarming experience, since the first thought to cross one's mind is that the growth may be malignant. Should it prove to be so, an operation must be carried out without delay, in the hope that the tumour can be removed before it has begun to spread throughout the body. A benign tumour will do no harm, but it too may have to be removed, depending on where it is sited or if it grows too large.

In a typical case, a Shih Tzu owner might notice a mammary tumour as a lump in one of a bitch's teats while carrying out routine grooming. This is one of those occasions when a quick visit to the vet is called for, and when the owner's powers of observation will prove invaluable. If the vet decides to operate to remove the lump immediately, he will be able to arrange for a pathological test to be carried out, to determine if the tumour is malignant or not.

Only tumours that appear on the surface of the dog's body can be detected by inspection during the grooming routine. Internal tumours grow hidden from view until their presence is revealed by such symptoms of illness as a digestive disorder.

The subject of tumours should not be too frightening. My own experience has been limited to two cases in the last ten years. The first concerned a bitch with a mammary tumour which proved to be malignant: because we found it very quickly it did not have time to spread to other parts of the body, and so after the removal of the lump our Twinkle lived on to a ripe old age with no recurrence. (Incidentally, a bitch that has been spayed after having one season is very unlikely to develop mammary tumours.) The second concerned a male, now sitting at my feet as I write, who had what I thought was a pimple to one side of his anus. It did not subside as a pimple should and turned out to be cancerous. In Ricky's case the treatment involved castration, as a result of which the tumour stopped growing, has reduced in size, and has so far given no more trouble.

Vomiting

Very occasionally, one or other of my Shih Tzus greets the day by throwing up a quantity of yellow, frothy fluid, a sign to me that he is what I call 'liverish', in other words has a case of mild indigestion. This may have been caused by over-eating, or by eating the wrong things, and is usually dealt with quite simply by means of a small dose of milk of magnesia. Fasting the dog for a day can also be beneficial in these circumstances, although water should not be withheld. When vomiting is repeated continually, or is accompanied by other symptoms, such as a fever or signs of pain or distress, seek veterinary advice.

Car sickness is most often reported by the owners of young puppies, and these often grow out of it before they are a year old. Any puppy will find the motion of a car and the whole experience of car travel exceedingly strange, so acclimatize him by taking him on frequent small excursions from an early age. One way to minimize the problem is to avoid feeding the dog before starting out, especially on a long journey. Car sickness medication that is marketed for human consumption should never be given to a dog.

Alternative Therapies

Several alternative therapies are used by dog owners nowadays, especially homoeopathy, herbalism and acupuncture. I have tried some of these over the years but never with enough success to convince me of their efficacy, and so I must confess to being somewhat sceptical. None the less, a number of Shih Tzu owners for whom I feel great respect have enormous faith in alternative remedies and assure me that they have used them with real success. It would make me uneasy if owners used alternative therapy instead of conventional veterinary treatment, but it is a different matter to use it in consultation with a qualified vet. For example, I recently heard of a Shih Tzu with a back problem, whose owner's vet also practised acupuncture. Although at first the diagnosis suggested the need for surgery, Joss was completely cured through the use of acupuncture over a period of several weeks.

There are a number of homoeopathic veterinary practitioners, and should you wish to find one the address of the British Association of Homoeopathic Veterinary Surgeons is given at the end of this book. In my list of suggestions for further reading I have also recommended a book on homoeopathic treatment for pets, which is both clearly written and full of common sense.

12

Shih Tzu Champions

Since Lady Brownrigg first made one of her dogs into a champion in 1949, more than 300 Shih Tzus have gained their titles in the UK. All of these had to win at least three CCs, under three different judges and against all-comers that included existing champions – a terrific achievement for their owners. Lack of space prevents me from describing each and every one of our British champions, so I have chosen to list those that have gained their titles in more recent years. I have included background information about some of these champions where I have been able to obtain it. Sometimes those who have yet to own a champion, or who keep their dogs purely as pets, regard these glamorous creatures as almost a breed apart, perhaps putting them up on a pedestal so they may be interested to know that the domestic behaviour of these famous dogs is no different from that of any other Shih Tzu.

A comment that I have heard repeatedly over the years from new exhibitors is that most of the new champions in any one year belong to a small group of well-known breeders, most of whom are themselves championship show judges. The implication is that there is some sort of cabal sharing the top awards among themselves, but the facts do not bear this out. First of all, it is to be expected that very experienced exhibitors will continue to enjoy a measure of success, or else they would hardly have persevered over twenty or thirty years, or more. On the other hand none of them was in this position when they won their first CC. In other words everyone has to start somewhere, and each year sees new exhibitors taking top awards for the first time, some of whom will go on to repeat this achievement year after year, whilst others will fail to follow up on their early success.

The number of shows in the years I have covered did not vary by more than one from year to year, yet it is interesting to note that the number of new champions differs quite considerably, with thirteen dogs gaining their titles in 1991 compared with only four in 1994.

1990

Ch. Cedarhythe Love 'N' Pride At Socorro   (by Harropine Cassidy of Huxlor out of Keltina Sun Princess of Cedarhythe), brindle/white dog, born in 1995, bred by Mrs Jenny Clifford and owned by Messrs Evans and Hutchins, whose first champion he was. I have reason to remember Ch. Cedarhythe Love 'N' Pride At Socorro, since I awarded him his third and qualifying CC at the BUBA Championship Show.

Ch. Chanikos Yu Kizzy of Tomolly   (by Lejusano Foo Wun out of Chanikos Oh Dianna), gold/white bitch, born 1988, bred by Mrs A. Spooner, owned by Mesdames Turner and Hennessey Smith, a first champion in the breed for both breeder and owners.

Ch. Crowvalley Anniversary   (by Ch. Crowvalley Pegasus out of Rosayleen Minstrel), black/white bitch, born 1986, bred by S. Fortun, owned by Mr and Mrs L. Williams.

Ch. Delbillie Cocoa The Clown   (by Ch. Santosha Royal Flush out of Lhakang Caprice), solid-gold dog, born 1987, bred and owned by Mr and Mrs Butterworth, their first champion.

Ch. Denroma Tiara At Tamanu   (by Paora Heza Ku-Tee out of Bellakerne Stacy Do), black/white bitch, bred by Mr D. Munford, owned by Mr and Mrs S. Ford and a first Shih Tzu champion for them.

Ch. Huxlor Escudos   (by Ch. Harropine Lord of The Rings out of Weatsom Pocket Money of Huxlor), grey/white dog, bred and owned by Mrs P. Lord in Somerset. This was the third champion from Mrs Pat Lord's Huxlor kennels, combining the well-known lines of Weatsom and Harropine. Pat's first champion, Ch. Harropine Super Trooper, came from the Harropine kennel.

Ch. Rosaril Delilah   (by Ch. Firefox of Santosha out of Ch. Rosaril Modesty Blaise), black/white bitch, born 1987, bred by Miss A. Stephenson, owned by Annabel's mother, Mrs E. Stephenson. In 1988 Eunice Stephenson had the distinction of gaining this title with one of the very few solid-black dogs to do it, Rosaril The Chimney Sweep.

Ch. Rossvale Pretty In Pink (by Ch. Keytor Any Questions out of Ch. Senousi Rosalita of Rossvale), gold/white bitch, born 1987, bred and owned by Mrs S. Brown.

Ch. Sueman Shihatzu Chaz At Emrose (by Mandabet Golden Dream out of Kizzy Wong), gold/white dog, born 1987, bred by Davies, owned by Mrs J. Howells.

Ch. Tatsanna The Charmer (by Kareth Kings Consort out of Tatsanna Shimmering Light), brindle/white dog, born 1987, bred by Scottish husband and wife team Dave and Anne Anderson, owned by Mrs Jean Lovely. Back in 1962, Jean made up the well-known Ch. Ellingham Kala Nag, Best of Breed at Crufts in both 1963 and 1964.

Ch. Wendolyn Wunda Wizard of Jardhu (by Ch. Santosha Sunking out of Wendolyn Wilma), solid-gold dog, born 1987, bred by Mrs W. Wood-Jones, owned by Mr and Mrs J. Grugan. Jim and Vicki Grugan are also from Scotland, and are keen exhibitors who probably dare not calculate the number of miles they have travelled up and down the British Isles in pursuit of their hobby but who have been rewarded for their enthusiasm with great success in the show ring. In 1990 their greatest triumph was yet to come (*see* Ch. Jardhu The Republican, 1994).

1991

Ch. Bowchild Promises Promises (by Ch. Firefox of Santosha out of Ch. Amylots Wai Wai Wonder), gold/white bitch, born 1987, bred and owned by Mrs P. Woodbridge.

Ch. Cedarhythe Lite My Fire (by Ch. Firefox of Santosha out of Sarosim Tseng Fwo At Cedarhythe), gold/white bitch, born 1987, bred by Mrs J. Clifford, owned by Messrs Carter and Donnaby.

Ch. Chelhama Pericles (by Ch. Chelhama Ajax Olympius out of Chelhama Persephone), black/white dog, born 1984, bred and owned by Mrs V. Goodwin. The Chelhama kennel is based in Kent, with no particular colour preference – Valerie Goodwin has made up seven champions in the last fifteen years, both black/white and gold/white.

Ch. Edsville Crackerjack (by Paora Wee Davie Baker out of Ta Mei of Edsville), gold/brindle/white dog, born 1987, bred and owned by Openshaw and Booth.

Ch. Grandavon Ming Toi (by Zuthis Bugsy Malone out of Prima Donna of Grandavon), gold/white bitch, born 1988, bred and owned by Mrs Y. Martin. (*See* colour section.)

Ch. Hashanah Hot Pursuit (by Ch. Weatsom Little Big Man of Hashanah out of Ch. Weatsom My Fair Lady of Hashanah), black/white dog, born 1989, bred and owned by Mrs J. Franks. Judy Franks, based in Birmingham, has enjoyed consistent success with her Hashanah Shih Tzus throughout the period under review. However, Hot Pursuit (winner of thirteen CCs) must remain among her best-known dogs, not least because it is rare for two dogs from the same litter to win as much in the show ring as did Hot Pursuit and his sister Ch. Hashanah Take Me To The Top. Of the two, my personal preference was for Take Me To The Top (*see* below), and many other judges also liked one better than the other.

Hashanah Take Me To The Top at the age of nine months.

Ch. Hashanah Take Me To The Top   (by Ch. Weatsom Little Big Man of Hashanah out of Ch. Weatsom My Fair Lady of Hashanah), black/white bitch, born 1989, bred and owned by Mrs J. Franks, and litter sister to the previous dog. Winner of the title of Top Shih Tzu in 1991 and 1992, she took eighteen CCs and also won the Utility group at championship shows on three occasions. (*See* colour section.)

Ch. Jardhu Myz-Sunn   (by Ch. Santosha Royal Flush out of Jardhu Mischievous Mi-Zee), gold/white dog, born 1988, bred and owned by Mr and Mrs J. Grugan.

Ch. Magique Magpie of Chelhama   (by King of Glory At Chelhama out of Leithill Lucinda), black/white bitch, born 1987, bred by Mrs Goodwin and Miss Cormack, owned by Mrs V. Goodwin.

Ch. Mingrovia Elite Petite of Tameron   (by Ch. Lhakang Cassius out of Mingrovia Madeline), gold/white bitch, born 1984, bred by Mrs C. Soulsby, owned by Mrs L. Howard. Linda Howard's first

Ch. Magique Magpie of Chelhama.

champion, 'Elite Petite' demonstrated admirably what lasting show dogs the Shih Tzus can be, for she gained her title as a veteran and was not the first in the breed to achieve this by any means.

Ch. Snaefells Limited Edition   (by Am. Ch. Din Ho Rupert T. Bear out of Snaefell Irma La Douce), gold/white dog, born 1988, bred and owned by Mrs A. L. Dadds. After more than thirty years in the breed, Audrey was innovative in seizing the opportunity to use as a sire this American dog, which was living for a time in England with his owner, Mrs J. Couch. Smaller and of a more refined type than many of the English males around at the time, Rupert also attracted Audrey on account of the lines in his pedigree.

Ch. Weatsom Madam Butterfly   (by Ch. Weatsom Tom Thumb At Cowley out of Weatsom Call Me Madam), gold/white bitch, born 1988, bred and owned by Mrs M. Stangeland. Margaret Stangeland's Devon-based kennel had its first champion in 1988.

Ch. Weatsom Tom Thumb At Cowley   (by Tom Fool of Keytor out of Marmalade Atkins At Tanzu), gold/brindle dog, born 1986, bred and owned by Mrs M. Stangeland.

1992

Ch. Bellakerne Misty Do   (by Zuthis Moonwalker out of Ch. Bellakerne Pagan Do), black/white bitch, born 1990, bred and owned by Mrs S. Richardson from Staffordshire. Tom and Sheila Richardson's first champion won her title in 1974, Ch. Patsy Do of Hyning (by Ch. Chin Ling of Greenmoss out of Hyning Lindi Lou, and bred by Mrs M. Rowling). Mary Rowling was looking for a name for the puppy and, as I recall the story, Sheila said 'Will Patsy do?' From this light-hearted suggestion came a stream of similar names for the Bellakerne kennel, including Ch. Bellakerne Zippity Do, Ch. Bellakerne Inca Do, Ch. Bellakerne Melissa Do and Int. Ch. Bellakerne Suki Sue, who gained her title in Sweden as well as in England.

Ch. Cabbala Beautiful Dreamer   (by Ch. Snaefell Limited Edition out of She Who Dares of Weatsom At Cabbala), grey/white bitch, born 1990, bred and owned by Mrs G. Goodwin. A first champion for her breeder, she was a granddaughter of Am. Ch. Din Ho Rupert T.

Bear through the Snaefell line, and won reserve Best in Show at the Blackpool Championship on the very day she won her first CC.

Ch. Chelhama De Courcey (by Ch. Firefox of Santosha out of Chelhama Persephone), gold/white dog, born 1988, bred and owned by Mrs V. Goodwin. (*See* colour section.) Although I greatly admire this lovely dog, I did not envy his owner the job of taking him in the ring, because he was very unpredictable and Val never knew quite what to expect of him, especially as a puppy. He more than once took it into his head to dance sideways instead of walking up the ring, and on occasions he was even known to roll over onto his back.

Ch. Greenmoss Praise Bee (by Ch. Camllien Touch of Class out of Greenmoss Daisy Tuo), gold/white bitch, born 1988. The latest in a long line of champions from the Greenmoss kennels, going back to 1964 (*see* Chapter 1).

Ch. Louwan Winning Colours At Huxlor (by Am. Ch. Louwans Rebel Rouser out of Am. Ch. Louwan Tootsie), gold and white dog, born in America in 1988, bred by Louis and Wanda Gec, and owned by Mrs P. Lord, who imported him from America. He was the first all-

Ch. Louwan Winning Colours At Huxlor (imported). (Photo: Steph Holbrook.)

American-bred male to become a British Champion, sired by a very well-known dog that has also produced 126 champions in America.

Ch. Meggy's Promise For Lharing   (by Yakee Grand Finale At Lharing out of Lharing Little Lady), gold bitch, born 1988, bred by Miss Meharry, owned by Mrs F. Harvie. Scotland has produced many enthusiastic Shih Tzu exhibitors, among them Tom and Freda Harvie of the Lharing kennel name. After Tom's untimely death, Freda decided to carry on showing, and Meggy's Promise was her third champion.

Ch. Snaefell Imperial Rose of Janmayen   (by Keltina Fan Kang of Snaefell out of Ch. Snaefell Imperial Imp), black/white bitch, born 1986, bred by Mrs A. Dadds, owned by Mesdames Pickburn and Duke. When she entered the Janmayen houshold Imperial Rose joined a family of Shih Tzu fanciers of long standing – both of Anne Pickburn's parents, Charles and Sheila Duke, are championship show judges of the breed, as is Anne herself. Anne and Sheila have owned and bred a number of champions in partnership over a long period.

Ch. Weatsom Dressed To Kill   (by Ch. Harropine China Town out of Weatsom Sugar & Spice), black/white bitch, born 1989, bred and owned by Mrs M. Stangeland.

Ch. Wendolyn Wildfire   (by Ch. Firefox of Santosha out of Ch. Wendolyn Wild Ginger), gold/white dog, born 1988, bred and owned by Mrs W. Wood-Jones. Wendy Wood-Jones has bred three champions, all of them sired by Santosha dogs, of which Wildfire is the second. The other two were sired by Ch. Santosha Sunking.

1993

Ch. Harropine Chasing Rainbows   (by Ch. Harropine China Town out of Dragonfires Scarlet O'Hara At Harropine), black/white bitch, born 1990, bred and owned by Mrs D. and Mr M. Harper. Dee Harper and her son Michael run a quarantine kennels in Devon, combining this with an enthusiasm for the Shih Tzu. They first found success showing a bitch from the Telota kennels of Mrs O. Newson, Ch. Telota Anouska. Their early stock was largely of the Telota and Antarctica lines. In recent years they have imported extensively from

America, and it will be interesting to see the long-term effects of combining these American lines with the English. Chasing Rainbows had a very successful show career, amassing no less than thirty-four CCs; yet her achievement is overshadowed by that of her kennel mate, Ch. Harropine Icarus (Ch. Santosha Sunking out of Harropine Thornbird) – a solid-gold/brindle dog that took over from Ch. Firefox of Santosha as the breed record holder by winning a total of thirty-five CCs. Ch. Harropine Icarus held this record until 1997.

Ch. Hashanah No Jacket Required   (by Ch. Weatsom Little Big Man of Hashanah out of Ch. Weatsom My Fair Lady of Hashanah), gold/white dog, born 1991, bred and owned by Mrs J. Franks. (*See* colour section.)

Ch. Hebouchon Wonder Woman   (by Ch. Santosha Sunking out of Stargem Yeh Ying), gold/white bitch, born 1989, bred and owned by Mr and Mrs C. Ripley, a first champion for her owners.

Ch. Hot Favourite At Huxlor   (by Basil Brush of The Gurnos out of Weatsom Glimpse of Gold), gold/white bitch, born 1988, bred by Mrs M. A. Hope, owned by Mrs P. Lord. The grandmother of Ch. Jardhu The Republican, this bitch has produced lovely puppies for Pat. She

Ch. Hot Favourite At Huxlor. (Photo: Steph Holbrook.)

has a particular mannerism of constantly touching her owner with a paw to draw attention to her needs, something she has passed on to her children.

Ch. Meikwei Happy Go Lucky   (by Kings Ransom For Lansu out of Patajohn Golden Sunshine), gold/white bitch, born 1986, bred and owned by Miss S. Brace, Sharon's first champion.

Ch. Santosha Chocolate Orange   (by Ch. Rosaril The Chimney Sweep out of Santosha Madame Butterfly of Phinjani), gold/white dog, born 1991, bred and owned by Mr and Mrs D. Crossley. (*See* colour section.) Sue and David Crossley, based at a boarding kennels in Shropshire, first gained a title with one of their Shih Tzus in the 1970s and have continued to campaign their dogs successfully ever since.

1994

Ch. Hashanah Just Like Kate   (by Bellakerne Brady of Erddig out of Ch. Weatsom My Fair Lady of Hashanah), black/white bitch, born 1989, bred and owned by Mrs J. Franks.

Ch. Jardhu The Republican   (by Bellakerne Dandi of Jardhu out of Huxlor Personality Plus of Jardhu), gold/white dog, born 1992, bred and owned by Jim and Vicky Grugan, the current breed record holder (*see* Chapter 7).

Ch. Keytor Luck Money   (by Zuthis Moonwalker out of Keytor Happy Returns), black/white bitch, born 1991, bred and owned by Mrs E. M. and Miss S. Johnson.

Ch. Rosaril Classical Jazz   (by Ch. Rosaril The Chimney Sweep out of Rosaril Painted Pony), gold bitch, born 1990, bred by Mrs S. Stephenson, owned by Mrs E. Stephenson.

1995

Ch. Cedarhythe Hot off The Press   (by Cedarhythe Call Me Boss out of Harropine Miss Bluebell of Cedarhythe), black-masked, solid-gold dog, born 1991, bred by Mrs J. Clifford and owned in partnership with Mr R. Edwards, although Jenny handled him in the ring herself.

Ch. Grandavon Orange Blossom of Delbillie   (by Superlion Warlord of Denroma out of Ch. Grandavon Ming Toi), gold/white bitch, born 1992, bred by Mrs Y. Martin, owned by Mrs D. W. Butterworth.

Ch. Harropine Scarlet Fever At Sealaw   (by Harropine Cleary out of Dragonfires Scarlet O'Hara At Harropine), black/white bitch, born 1994, bred by Mrs D. and Mr M. Harper, owned by Mr G. Corish.

Ch. Hashanah Tuff At The Top   (by Ch. Greenmoss Praise Bee out of Ch. Weatsom My Fair Lady of Hashanah), gold/white bitch, born 1992, bred and owned by Mrs J. Franks.

Ch. Keytor Say No More   (by Keytor True Love out of Keytor Happy Returns), gold/white dog, born 1993, bred and owned by Mrs E. M. and Miss S. Johnson.

Ch. Peekin Tashi-Tu   (by Kuire William Wagtail out of Fernell Kerrygold Girl At Peekin), gold/white bitch, born 1991, bred and owned

Ch. Grandavon Orange Blossom of Delbillie.

by Mr and Mrs N. Stevens. (*See* colour section.) Sandra and Nigel have tended to concentrate on gold/white in their breeding programme. Tashi-Tu, the result of a third repeat mating of her sire and dam, is the grandmother of Ch. Peekin Sophie-Tu and shares with her the enviable characteristic of having pure white whiskers which never get stained. She loves showing but does not care to wait for her turn in the ring in a cage, so her special friend, Sheila Rabson, carries her around in her arms at most shows to keep her entertained.

Ch. Santosha Red October   (by Furaha Feu De Lion out of Santosha Mistle Thrush), solid-gold dog, born 1993, bred and owned by Mr and Mrs D. Crossley. (*See* colour section.)

Ch. Tameron Miss Finesse   (by Benjamin of Lhakang out of Ch. Mingrovia Elite Petite of Tameron), gold/white bitch, born 1987, bred and owned by Mrs L. Howard.

Ch. Weatsom Concorde of Berylendan   (by Bosley Goes To Weatsom out of Weatsom A Dream Come True), black/white dog, born 1989, bred by Mrs M. Stangeland, owned by Miss E. L. Gibbons, and her first champion.

Ch. Weatsom New Beginnings   (by Furaha Ephesus of Weatsom out of Weatsom Sugar And Spice), black/white dog, born 1990, bred and owned by Mrs M. Stangeland.

1996

Ch. Emrose Michelin Man   (by Sistasu Silver Bullion At Trakay out of Surprise Packet At Emrose), black/white dog, born 1993, bred and owned by Mrs J. Howells. (*See* colour section.)

Ch. Grandavon Georgie Girl of Balise   (by Superlion Warlord of Denroma out of Ch. Grandavon Ming Toi), gold/white bitch, born 1992, bred by Mrs Y. Martin, owned by Mrs I. and Miss P. Malcolm, a first champion for her owners.

Ch. Harropine Frill A Minute   (by Harropine Cleary out of Dragonfires Scarlet O'Hara At Harropine), black/white bitch, born 1995, bred and owned by Mrs D. and Mr M. Harper.

Ch. Hashanah Relentless Pursuit (by Ch. Hashanah Hot Pursuit out of Ch. Hashanah Just Like Kate), gold/white dog, born 1994, bred and owned by Mrs J. Franks. (*See* colour section.)

Ch. Hashanah The Immaculate (by Ch. Greenmoss Praise Bee out of Ch. Hashanah Take Me To The Top), black/white bitch, born 1994, bred and owned by Mrs J. Franks. (*See* page 209.)

Ch. Honeybun Maiden of Chelhama (by Ch. Chelhama Pericles out of Misty's Melody Maker), black/white bitch, born 1991, bred by Mrs J. Humphreys, owned by Mrs V. Goodwin.

Ch. Huxlor He's A Rebel (by Louwan Rebel Tu At Huxlor out of Ch. Hot Favourite At Huxlor), brindle/white dog, born 1990, bred and owned by Mrs P. Lord.

Ch. Metadale Mungojerrie (by Ch. Firefox of Santosha out of Metadale Starlight Express), gold/white dog, born 1993, bred and owned by Mr R. Metcalfe. (*See* colour section.) Roy Metcalfe was involved in the breed for many years and was well known as the

Hashanah The Immaculate as a puppy.

Ch. Honeybun Maiden of Chelhama. (Photo: Sue Domun.)

officer of one of the breed clubs, but had done very little exhibiting before he decided to campaign this dog. 'Mac', as he is known at home, gained his title in record time, with only a matter of weeks between winning his first and third CCs. He has also won Best in Show more than once. His breeder particularly values him for his outgoing personality, which he is passing on to his puppies.

Ch. Sannajae Chocolate Charmer (by Ch. Santosha Chocolate Orange out of Shihfon Chelsea), solid-gold dog, born 1993, bred and owned by Mrs D. Shepherd, her first champion.

Ch. Treeoo Trooping The Colours (by Harropine Eclipse of The Sun At Treeoo out of Harropine China Chimes For Treeoo), gold/white dog, born 1993, bred and owned by Mr and Mrs Gibbons.

Ch. Weatsom Brandy Snap (by Ch. Weatsom Tom Thumb At Cowley out of Weatsom Dressed For Success), grey dog, born 1994, bred and owned by Mrs M. Stangeland.

Ch. Weatsom Dressed For April (by Ch. Weatsom Tom Thumb At Cowley out of Weatsom Dressed For Success), black/white bitch, born 1994, bred and owned by Mrs M. Stangeland.

1997/8

Ch. Bellakerne Sharnie-Do (by Whitethroat Chinese Tiger out of Ch. Bellakerne Misty Do), black/white bitch, born 1994, bred and owned by Mrs S. Richardson.

Ch. Chelhama Dry Ginger (by Chelhama Going For Gold out of Mahneldene Meorny), gold/white dog, born 1994, bred and owned by Mrs V. Goodwin.

Ch. Domela A-Ming-Hi (by Weatsom Huggy Bear At Chadris out of Delmarvey Queen Bee of Domela), black/white bitch, born 1992, bred and owned by Mrs P. Bickers, a first champion for his owner.

Ch. Superlion Jefferson.

Ch. Peekin Sophie-Tu (by Ch. Santosha Red October out of Peekin Kochia), gold/white bitch, born 1995, bred and owned by Mr and Mrs N. Stevens. (*See* colour section.)

Ch. Superlion Jefferson (by Pause For Applause At Shalihi out of Berylendans Belladene), gold/white dog, born 1992, bred and owned by Mrs L. A. Leon, her first champion in the breed. (*See* page 210.)

Ch. Wynele Sing Linnet Sing (by Peekin Tobias out of Wynele Chantill Leala), gold/white bitch, born 1995, bred and owned by Messrs Barker and Naulls, their first Shih Tzu champion. Linnet loves to go to shows and at home she is equally the show-off, demanding attention from Nigel on all occasions. When he is on the telephone she will stand on her hind legs and bark very loudly, an effective way to curtail the conversation. She is descended from the Kuire line through her father.

Ch. Wynele Sing Linnet Sing.

Redhall Harvey Moon, aged six weeks.

Ch. Redhall Harvey Moon.

Ch. Huxlor Gino Ginelli (by Harropine Columbus out of Har-ropine Mona Lisa), red/white dog, born 1992, bred and owned by Mrs P. Lord. (*See* colour section.) Pat describes Gino Ginelli as having been slow to mature, something she finds common in her stock. She says he is a charming dog to live with, whose happiness at home depends on his collection of cuddly toys.

Ch. Redhall Harvey Moon (by Peekin Tobias out of Lady Tan Kai Lulubelle At Redhall), gold/white dog, born 1992, bred and owned by Mrs G. C. Townsin. (*See* page 212.) Gloria says that Harvey has never been easy to show, setting off at top speed and generally being a pickle to handle. At home he is always on the go, and is not one to sit on her lap for long. Harvey is another dog to whom toys are an important part of life, and he never greets Gloria upon her return to the house without bringing her a toy as a present. He loves his food, and has been a very happy and contented dog since puppyhood.

In order to list all the world's Shih Tzu champions, I should need to write another book. However, this sample (taken from just one country over the span of a few years) illustrates the points that any such list would show. We can see how some breeders become pre-eminent by producing a series of champions. After years of such success, their kennel names gain such a high profile that they acquire an international reputation. In this way I have become familiar with, for example, such names as Chumulari, Dragonwyck and Louwan in America, and Geltree and Mudan in Australia, even though I have never visited these countries. Thus it was that the names of Taishan and Lhakang – with which I began my book – became so very famous.

Just as every dog is a champion to his loving owner, it can be judged from the remarks volunteered by some of the champion owners that their successful show dogs are also much-loved pets. This is especially worthy of note, for it has been my intention throughout this book to stress that the Shih Tzu is a very special little dog, deserving of as privileged a place in our homes today as he once occupied in the imperial palaces of ancient China.

Appendices

I: British Breed Standard 1958–86

General Appearance

Very active, lively and alert, with a distinctly arrogant carriage. The Shih Tzu is neither a terrier nor a toy dog.

Head and Skull

Head broad and round, wide between the eyes. Shock-headed, with hair falling well over the eyes. Good beard and whiskers, the hair growing upwards on the nose giving a distinctly chrysanthemum-like effect. Muzzle square and short, but not wrinkled like a Pekingese, flat and hairy. Nose black for preference and about 1in (2.5cm) from tip to stop.

Eyes

Large, dark and round but not prominent.

Ears

Large, with long leathers, and carried drooping. Set slightly below the crown of the skull; so heavily coated that they appear to blend with the hair of the neck.

Mouth

Level or slightly underhung.

Forequarters

Legs short and muscular with ample bone. The legs should look massive on account of the wealth of hair.

Body

Body between withers and root of tail should be longer than height at withers; well-coupled and sturdy; chest broad and deep, shoulders firm, back level.

Hindquarters

Legs short and muscular with ample bone. They should look straight when viewed from the rear. Thighs well-rounded and muscular. Legs should look massive on account of the wealth of hair.

Feet

Firm and well-padded. They should look big on account of the wealth of hair.

Tail

Heavily plumed, curled well over back; carried gaily, set on high.

Coat

Long and dense, but not curly, with good undercoat.

Colour

All colours permissable, but a white blaze on the forehead and a white tip to the tail are highly prized. Dogs with liver markings have dark liver noses and slightly lighter eyes. Pigmentation on muzzle as unbroken as possible.

Weight and Size

Up to 18lb (8.2kg) ideal weight 9–16lb (4.1–7.3kg). Height at withers not more than 10in (12.5cm). Type and breed characteristics of the greatest importance and on no account to be sacrificed to size alone.

Faults

Narrow heads, pig jaws, snipeyness, pale pink noses and eye rims, small or light eyes, legginess, sparse coat.

Note: Male animals should have two apparently normal testicles fully descended into the scrotum.

II: Crufts Winners 1968–98

Winners of Challenge Certificates at Crufts over thirty years, listed year by year. In each case the winning dog precedes the bitch.

1968	Ch. Antarctica Chan Shih of Darite
	Ch. Ling Fu of Antarctica
1969	Ch. Fleeting Yu SiFng of Antarctica
	Ch. Yuh Chin Wong
1970	Ch. Jen Kai Ko of Lhakang
	Ch. Che-Ko of Antarctica
1971	Ch. Dominic of Telota
	Dapperlee Yokima
1972	Ch. Chin Ling of Greenmoss
	Ch. Fei Ying of Greenmoss
1973	Ch. Kuire Hermes of Antarctica
	Ch. Cherholmes Golden Samantha
1974	Ch. Greenmoss Gideon
	Ch. Elfann Golden Posy of Lansu
1975	Crowvalley Yenisi
	Ch. Santosha Rambling Rose
1976	Ch. Meriadoc Kahedin
	Ch. Su Tung P'o of Antarctica
1977	Ch. Crowvalley Tweedledum
	Ch. Keytor Sweet Charity
1978	Ch. Montzella's Tsi Chou
	Ch. Shou Shang of Antarctica
1979	Ch. Bellakerne Zippity Do
	Ch. Bellakerne Inca Do
1980	Ch. Crowvalley Tweedledum
	Ch. Tercero's Enchantress
1981	Ch. Wentres Jay Cee Valencee
	Ch. Queensfield Tutsi Wong of Chelhama
1982	Ch. Emrose Spinning Wheel
	Ch. Kareth Khoir Angel
1983	Ch. Wentres Jay Cee Valencee
	Ch. Greenmoss Surely Bee
1984	Ch. Santosha Sunking
	Ch. Montzellas Rosa Lin
1985	Ch. Jardhu Waffles Wu
	Ch. Harropine Christmas Carol

1986	Ch. Keytor Any Questions
	Keltina Kou Ling
1987	Ch. Harropine Chaka Khan at Antarctica
	Ch. Senousi Be Bop Delux
1988	Ch. Firefox of Santosha
	Ch. Santosha Tiger Lily
1989	Ch. Harropine Chaka Khan at Antarctica
	Ch. Amylots Wai-Wai Wonder
1990	Ch. Sebastian of Keytor
	Ch. Chanikos Yu Kizzy of Tomolly
1991	Ch. Firefox of Santosha
	Ch. Weatsom Madam Butterfly
1992	Ch. Harropine Icarus
	Ch. Hashanah Take Me To The Top
1993	Bellakerne Rory-Do at Lharing
	Ch. Bellakerne Misty-Do
1994	Ch. Harropine Icarus
	Sarosim Kung Chu
1995	Ch. Santosha Chocolate Orange
	Hashanah Tuff at the Top
1996	Glentoth Last Chance For Chadris
	Ch. Peekin Tashi-Tu
1997	Ch. Emrose Michelin Man
	Ch. Hashanah The Immaculate
1998	Kevelles Alive 'N' Kicking
	Ch. Peekin Sophie-Tu

Useful Addresses

Details of local and regional breed clubs can be obtained from the national kennel clubs.

The Kennel Club of Great Britain
1 Clarges Street
London W1Y 8AB

The American Kennel Club
51 Madison Avenue
New York
NY 10010

Australian National Kennel Council
Royal Show Grounds
Ascot Vale
3032 Victoria

Kennel Union of Southern Africa
6th Floor, Bree Castle
68 Bree Street
Cape Town 8001
South Africa

Shih Tzu Club
Hon. Sec. Mrs J. Johnson
Holmcroft
Brook Road
Bassingbourn
Royston
Herts
SG8 5NT

Manchu Shih Tzu Society
Hon. Sec. Mrs V. Goodwin
Collards
Bexon Lane
Bredgar
Sittingbourne
Kent
ME9 8HD

Northern Counties Shih Tzu Club
Hon. Sec. Mr R. Metcalfe
Metadale
High Moor Top
Cononley
Near Keighley
Yorkshire
BD20 8PD

Shih Tzu Club of Wales & South West
Hon. Sec. Mrs D. Harding
Ithaca
Newbury Road
Baydon
Near Marlborough
Wiltshire
SN8 2JF

Shih Tzu Club of Scotland
Hon. Sec. Mrs V. Grugan
Friarside
Cessnock Road
Galston
Ayrshire
KA4 8LR

Ulster Shih Tzu Club
Hon. Sec. Mrs. I. Cummings
10 Crawford Park
Belfast
BT6 9RS

Internationaler Shih Tzu Club e.V.
Vorsitzende Frau Linda Reinelt-Gebauer
Weiherstrasse 2
57629 Steinebach a. d. Wied
Germany

British Association of Homoeopathic Veterinary Surgeons
Chinham House
Stanford-in-the Vale
Faringdon
Oxfordshire
SN7 8NQ

Further Reading

Billinghurst, Dr Ian, *Give Your Dog A Bone*, Abbeywood Publishing (1993).

Bloomfield, Betty, *Nursing and Hand Rearing Newborn Puppies*, Able Publishing, Knebworth (1994).

Collier, V. W. F., *Dogs of China and Japan in Nature and Art*, Heinemann (1921).

Dadds, A. L., *Shih Tzu*, Kingdom Books (1995).

Evans, J. M., & White, Kay, *The Doglopaedia*, Henston Ltd. (1985).

Frankling, Eleanor, *Practical Dog Breeding and Genetics*, Popular Dogs Publishing Co. Ltd. (1961).

Gurney, Dorothy, *Pet Owners Guide to the Shih Tzu*, Ringpress Books Ltd. (1994).

Hunter, Francis, *Homeopathic First Aid Treatment for Pets*, Thorsons (1988).

Laufer, Berthold, *Chinese Pottery of the Han Dynasty*, Charles E. Tuttle, Japan (1962).

Smythe, R. H., *The Anatomy of Dog Breeding*, Popular Dogs Publishing Co. Ltd. (1962).

Widdrington, Gay, *The Shih Tzu Handbook*, privately published (1971).

Index